Bernard Shaw's *The Black Girl in Search of God*

The Florida Bernard Shaw Series

Florida A&M University, Tallahassee
Florida Atlantic University, Boca Raton
Florida Gulf Coast University, Ft. Myers
Florida International University, Miami
Florida State University, Tallahassee
University of Central Florida, Orlando
University of Florida, Gainesville
University of North Florida, Jacksonville
University of South Florida, Tampa
University of West Florida, Pensacola

THE FLORIDA BERNARD SHAW SERIES
Edited by R. F. Dietrich

*This series was made possible by a generous grant
from the David and Rachel Howie Foundation.*

"Hiding green thoughts in green shade." Farleigh's cover design for *The Black Girl*. Reproduced by permission of The Society of Authors, on behalf of the Bernard Shaw Estate.

Bernard Shaw's
The Black Girl in Search of God

The Story behind the Story

Leon Hugo

University Press of Florida

Gainesville · Tallahassee · Tampa · Boca Raton
Pensacola · Orlando · Miami · Jacksonville · Ft. Myers

08 07 06 05 04 03   6 5 4 3 2 1

Library of Congress Cataloging-in-Publication Data
Hugo, Leon.
Bernard Shaw's The black girl in search of God : the story
behind the story / Leon Hugo.
p. cm. — (The Florida Bernard Shaw Series)
Includes bibliographical references and index.
ISBN 0-8130-2626-1
1. Shaw, Bernard, 1856–1950. Adventures of the black girl
in search of God. 2. Women, Black, in literature. 3. Religion
in literature. 4. God in literature. I. Title. II. Series.
PR5365.A42H84 2003
822'.912—dc21   2003047335

The University Press of Florida is the scholarly publishing
agency for the State University System of Florida, comprising
Florida A&M University, Florida Atlantic University, Florida
Gulf Coast University, Florida International University, Florida
State University, University of Central Florida, University
of Florida, University of North Florida, University of South
Florida, and University of West Florida.

University Press of Florida
15 Northwest 15th Street
Gainesville, FL 32611–2079
http://www.upf.com

Contents

Illustrations

following page 59

Foreword

Much of Bernard Shaw's effort was directed toward breaking people of bad habits he thought destructive. His famous fable, *The Adventures of the Black Girl in Search of God*, was precisely aimed at breaking people of certain *religious* habits he thought destructive. If it hadn't been for one of his own bad habits, however, that fable might never have been written, and the case illustrates the Shavian point that bad habits often start out well intentioned and thus require special consciousness-raising to overcome, for it is hard to see past good as present bad.

Perhaps the most immediate inspiration for the writing of *The Black Girl* was in a past good habit turning sour on Shaw, if we can count learning to drive a car as a good. It seems Shaw had learned to drive on a 1908 DeDietrich, an automobile now thought peculiar in its arrangement of the brake pedal on the right and gas pedal on the left. Thus in later years when driving cars with the present opposite arrangement, Shaw sometimes out of old habit stepped on the gas when he meant to press on the brake. The most notorious example occurred when visiting South Africa in 1932, on the road from Cape Town to Port Elizabeth. Overconfidently speeding down a relatively straight stretch of road until a bump sent him violently to the left, he overcorrected with a swerve to the right and, instead of braking, unintentionally accelerated through a ditch, a hedge, a fence, and so on. While his bruised and battered wife spent several weeks recuperating in a nearby hotel, an inspired Shaw wrote his fable about the need to forcibly break bad habits, which he considered especially important for those who would steer civilization and who thus need to be awake to danger.

Enlightenment often begins, Shaw thought, with awakening to the realization that a good habit has turned bad. His examples in *The Black*

Girl are from the world's religions (or religious philosophy), all of which may have started out with good intentions long ago, but which to Shaw seemed to be running on automatic pilot, with the people in charge stepping thoughtlessly on the gas just when they should be braking. It would take an independent-minded person looking freshly at things to see the crash that was coming if people were to continue automatically with present religious beliefs. To embody the sort of fresh, wide-awake thinking needed, Shaw created one of the most unlikely heroines of a British fable, the African Black Girl, who, less encumbered by Western habits of thinking (not to mention Western clothes!), is unsatisfied with programmed answers to religious questions, and who thus, during her search for God, cracks her knobkerry over the heads of all the automatic pilots of traditional religion she meets to wake them up from their snooze. Not that it does much good. They soon go back to their zombie ways, and she is forced to conclude that the best she can do is leave them to their folly and cultivate her own garden, à la Voltaire, after realizing that God is not something to be sought but a presence to be felt at one's elbow as one does the obvious work that needs to be done. By the end of the fable, she has married a red-bearded Irishman to do the digging in the garden and give her children to raise, both doing God's work, as it were. It was always Shaw's hope that the young women he spent so much time educating would bring their children up more wisely, and therefore it's not surprising that this fable ends as so many of his stories do, with an enlightened young woman passing her enlightenment on.

This is just one of many facets of the fascinating story of how Shaw came to write *The Black Girl*, what its antecedents were, what elements make it up, what reactions ensued, and so forth. Here for the first time we have the whole story thoroughly recounted by Leon Hugo, a South African, well-known Shaw scholar, and formerly professor emeritus at the University of South Africa, in a manner most appropriate to perhaps the most charming work Shaw ever penned. One of the things Professor Hugo reveals is that even some of those who took this fable as a grenade lobbed into their bunkers appreciated this charm and ultimately forgave the bomber. This throwing of charming bombs was by 1932 an old habit of Shaw's, but whether good or bad by then, he couldn't break himself of the habit.

Of course, some habits we are forced to break. Sadly, as this book was making its way through the publishing process, news came that Leon

Hugo had died. And so Shaw Studies will have now to break itself of an old habit, that of looking to Leon Hugo for such sterling work as this book, which nevertheless stands as a final testament to all his fine qualities as a man and a scholar. We thank Leon's children, especially Pippa, for their overseeing the transformation of manuscript into page proofs, and hope that they will find some solace in having made this contribution to their father's final say.

R. F. Dietrich
27 October 2002

Acknowledgments

As usual, my thanks and appreciation go to Shavians worldwide, whose interest and encouragement are never stinted. Thanks in particular to the following scholars and institutions without whose assistance, guidance, and advice this book could not have been written:

Stanley Weintraub, who first suggested *The Black Girl* as a topic in Shavian studies to me, and whose support by way of encouragement and practical input has been considerable.

Dan H. Laurence, whose storehouse of knowledge has always been open to Shavian scholars and who has here been instrumental in opening up several avenues of inquiry.

Michel W. Pharand, who made the Voltairean pages of his book *Shaw and the French* available to me before publication, and whose contribution to chapter 1, "Antecedents," is greater than the text reveals.

Cecelia Zeiss, whose research into and inquiries regarding various religious issues greatly eased and clarified my task.

Tony Gibbs, for sharing his insights into *The Black Girl* with me.

Charles Berst, who tracked down the text—a rare item—of Durrell's *Bromo Bombastes.*

The Society of Authors, in particular the head of copyright, Jeremy Crow, for permission to quote text and use illustrations held in copyright by the Bernard Shaw Estate; also for providing information about adaptations and readings of *The Black Girl* by the BBC and other institutions and persons.

The BBC Written Archives Centre at Cavendish Park, Reading, for permission to cite material in the Bernard Shaw files.

The archivist of the University of Guelph Library, who made available several rare texts in the Dan H. Laurence Collection.

The interlibrary loan department of the Library of the University of South Africa; the South African State Library; the British Library, particularly the Newspaper Library at Colindale, all of which provided exemplary service.

Susan Hussey, for her report on the production of *The Black Girl* by her husband, Aubrey Hampton.

The staff of the University Press of Florida, Amy Gorelick in particular, whose advice and kindly assistance are greatly appreciated.

Last and by no means least, Richard Dietrich, general editor of the Bernard Shaw Series of the University Press of Florida, for his encouragement and advice.

1

Antecedents

Voltaire and Others

Shaw wrote his allegory *The Adventures of the Black Girl in Her Search for God*—to give the work its full original title—in February to March 1932 in a hotel room in Knysna, a coastal resort in the eastern Cape, South Africa, while his wife Charlotte was recovering from injuries sustained in a motor accident.[1] In a later chapter, I will give a full account of the events that led to this, but the circumstances were so out of the ordinary, so much a dislocation of the ordered tenor of Shaw's and Charlotte's lives, that a preliminary explanation is called for.

They went on holiday to South Africa in 1932, arriving in Cape Town on the *Carnarvon Castle* on Monday, 11 January of that year.[2] As was Shaw's habit—as was his compulsion—he adhered to his regimen of work on board ship, producing in the eighteen or so days of the passage from Southampton some forty pages of a new project, a monograph provisionally titled "The Rationalization of Russia." He probably intended completing this during his visit to South Africa, and it is highly unlikely that he entertained any notion when he disembarked of abandoning the project or of producing a religious allegory instead.[3]

Yet this is what happened. Russia was gradually jettisoned and would never be rationalized in print by Shaw himself (although he used the material he had at hand in his public address in the Cape Town city hall on 1 February 1932). And while Russia fell away, *The Black Girl in Search of God* superseded it, claimed precedence over other Shavian commitments, thrust itself into Shaw's consciousness, and insisted on coming into being. It was the motor accident that brought this about.

Shaw and Charlotte, accompanied on the South African leg of their intended journey by Commander C. P. Newton of the Cape Town Publicity Bureau, left Cape Town on 7 February to travel to Port Elizabeth, where they intended to board ship to return home along the east coast of Africa. They progressed by easy stages until the morning of 10 February, when Shaw, who was driving, lost control and the car veered off the road into the "veld"—not, as he later insisted, "into a ditch." He and Newton were shaken but not injured; Charlotte was badly injured, and recuperative bed rest was ordered for her at a hotel in the nearby hamlet of Knysna, three hundred miles from Cape Town, nearly two hundred miles from Port Elizabeth.

Stuck in this backwater, knowing that Charlotte would need some weeks in which to recover, Shaw turned his mind to (as he put it) "the ordinary course of my business as a playwright"—but "found myself writing the story of the black girl instead."

It seems to have been a spontaneous decision, and he himself declared in his afterword—the preface in later editions—that he was "inspired" to write the book.[4] Be this as it may (and the question of "inspiration" will be considered in chapter 6), it was not spontaneous. Nothing is truly so, and while the trauma of the motor accident and all that followed could well have induced a lapsing away from the set pattern of Shaw's working agenda, the greater effect of the trauma would have been catalytic. This, given the situation in which he and Charlotte abruptly and violently found themselves, would have brought back to his conscious mind apparently disparate unrelated influences, events, and experiences of both the remote and the recent past that, duly processed by the creative imagination, would become an ordered, unified entity and would coalesce as the finished work, his story of the Black Girl. It was all there, a jumble of impulses waiting to be shocked into order and to declare themselves as the imperative of the moment.

So there Shaw was, in this little town looking out on a picturesque lagoon with dense coastal forest looming over it, writing his allegory. One may imagine him at work there as this discussion turns to some antecedent issues and influences—the more remote ones first—that directed his mind and pen.

The first and most important consideration is that the primary theme of *The Black Girl* is religious. This is no surprise in itself. A significant proportion of Shaw's writings—his plays, prefaces, pamphlets, and postscripts—is religious, often overtly as in *Major Barbara* or *Back to Methuselah* or *Saint Joan,* usually implicitly, as in almost everything else he wrote. The surprise is that he should revert to religious themes he had dealt with twenty years before, in his preface to *Androcles and the Lion*, for instance. *The Black Girl* is therefore something of an anachronism, particularly in the context of the political issues Shaw had been making his own in the late 1920s and early 1930s. There must have been a reason for this reversion, and there was; rather, there were plenty of reasons, some of which I will discuss in chapter 2.

The Black Girl is also a literary freak. Taking the form of the classic quest, or journey of discovery, there is nothing else quite like it within Shaw's body of work. One may argue that quite a number of Shaw's female protagonists embark on "quests," usually of self-discovery—like Eliza Doolittle—but this is to use the term loosely, whereas the Black Girl's quest is rooted in the immemorial tradition of Western literature, going as far back as Jason and the Argonauts, for example, and continuing with the quest literature of the Middle Ages through the Renaissance and on to its mutations in the picaresque quests of more recent literary ages. These are the antecedents of *The Black Girl*, and plainly the work is not sui generis. But it is unique in Shaw, isolated by its form from its companions in the oeuvre.

Shaw was steeped in the Western literary tradition to an extent he did not usually reveal. These writers were part of his intellectual equipment, informing his work in unexpected and surprising ways, as though he were enjoying a private joke at the expense of an unenlightened multitude. Though no classicist, he knew the classics well, and one need do no more than glance at the titles and themes of some of his major works to detect their origins in the masterpieces of ancient Greece and Rome. There is *Arms and the Man*, with its echoes of Virgil's *Aeneid*, and *Major Barbara*, rooted in the *Bacchae* of Euripides; *Pygmalion* derives from the well-known myth, and *Androcles and the Lion* rests on an equally well known and loved tale. Then there are other derivations, playful echoes, as in the names of the characters in *The Apple Cart*—Proteus, Pliny, Crassus, Lysistrata, Boanerges (Hebrew rather than classical), and so on—all aimed at imparting resonance, often ironic, to the work in question.

What about *The Black Girl*, one may ask? Are there classical antecedents here, apart from the quest theme? There seem to be one or two at least in the heroine herself. She could, and perhaps should, be regarded as Shaw's updated 1930s model of the Greek goddess Athena (Minerva in Roman mythology), worshiped and venerated in different parts and times of the classical world as the goddess of war—not as a warrior so much as a leader of warriors—and as the goddess of the arts and handicrafts, particularly as the patroness of women's work. As the daughter of Metis, the personification of wise counsel, Athena would also have possessed wisdom. The principal myth concerning her is her birth: Zeus, fearing that his wife, Metis, would give birth to a son mightier than he, swallowed her whole; Hephaestus or some other violently inclined deity split open Zeus's head, and Athena sprang forth, fully armed and uttering her war cry.

There does not seem anything here to connect her with the Black Girl, but a few parallels emerge: the Black Girl may not be warlike, but she—like Athena—is armed, and she is more than ready to apply her knobkerry where corrective blows are called for. Her quest halted at Voltaire's cottage, she readily puts her knobkerry aside and turns to a Voltairean version of handicrafts, that is, tilling the earth—later motherhood and housekeeping—rather than spinning and weaving; so perhaps a touch of Athena's other occupation enters here. And she is certainly wise beyond her years. An intriguing, if rather insubstantial, parallel is in the birth of each. The Black Girl, like Athena, sprang from the mind of her creator. It is a tenuous link, but Shaw, for once, seems to provide a clue as to his intention: in 1934, he reengaged John Farleigh, the illustrator of *The Black Girl*, to produce a wood engraving for the title page of *Prefaces of Bernard Shaw*, published by Constable of London in that year. The central image of Farleigh's illustration—and if this was not prompted by Shaw, it was certainly approved by him—is of Shaw himself, with the Black Girl issuing from his head á la Zeus and Athena.

This is not all. The Black Girl in her role as Athena emerges strongly as a champion of several causes built into the tale, as will emerge in the account that follows.

To move to comparatively recent times, an important model was John Bunyan's *Pilgrim's Progress*, the English touchstone of the religious quest (or pilgrimage) residing in allegory. Bunyan was a major figure in Shaw's "apostolic succession," that is, writers with a mission to better the world, and it was inevitable that his masterpiece should enter the pages of *The Black Girl*, albeit ironically in that the absolute biblical certainties that guide Christian in his progress to the Heavenly City are rejected in the Black Girl's quest. The affinities go beyond this, as Shaw himself refers to the Caravan of the Curious—those unlovely men and women the

Black Girl meets in the forest—as being modeled on Bunyan's jury in the Vanity Fair interlude of his book.

Of all other antecedent literary works, far and away the most important and obvious is Voltaire's *Candide;* also, perhaps more obviously, Voltaire himself, who takes his position center stage toward the end of the Black Girl's quest. Before considering Voltaire, or more precisely, his relation to Shaw, I will look first at *Candide*—the book and its eponymous hero—as a forerunner of *The Black Girl*, the book and its eponymous heroine.

At first glance the two works seem more unalike than alike. *Candide* is eighteenth-century in form. It is episodic if not strictly picaresque, depicting a pilgrimage of a kind, if not consciously a quest, and the events that constitute the story are held together by a series of calamities that are Voltaire's rebuttal of Leibniz and Rousseau's belief that everything that happens is for the best in the best of all possible worlds. Candide, the "Optimist," the innocent at large, does not act; he is acted upon, the victim—together with various companions, Pangloss and the beauteous, and later the exceedingly ugly Cunégonde—of a fate as arbitrary as it is cruel. *The Black Girl* is also eighteenth-century in form, though more firmly constructed than *Candide;* it is also episodic, though better developed than *Candide;* also a pilgrimage, though the heroine's adventures are altogether gentler than the unbridled horrors that beset Candide. And where Candide is buffeted by misfortune, the Black Girl, armed with her stout knobkerry, is more than capable of protecting herself and engaging in occasional corrective buffeting on her own account. It is an important distinction, for while Candide's adventures illustrate Voltaire's belief that suffering is an inescapable condition of life no matter how doggedly one seeks "happiness," the Black Girl's adventures illustrate Shaw's belief that the dedicated soul can and must transcend Voltaire's tragic vision. To survive, the twentieth-century pilgrim has to repudiate it and apply personal initiative and derring-do, like his Black Girl, to reach for and perhaps find God. In making this distinction—in advancing beyond Voltairean "reality"—Shaw evades the question of suffering (and does not introduce it in his depiction of Voltaire in *The Black Girl*), but he also suggests that in the twentieth-century world meek submission to fate is the craven's way out. As his twentieth-century Joan had said not many years before, "I will dare, and dare, and dare, until I die" to achieve the eventual triumph of the human spirit.

Yet overall, in spite of these differences, *Candide* and *The Black Girl* are cast in the same spiritual mold. Each writer in his way in these particular books—Voltaire in the eighteenth century, Shaw in the twentieth—denounces and tries to demolish received religious (and philosophical) beliefs. Scorn was their starting point, satire their means, skepticism the shared outlook. If in the end Shaw hauls *Candide* into the twentieth century while modernizing its theological principles in accordance with Shavian faith, his book remains the same as Voltaire's, holding institutionalized religion and half-baked philosophy up to ridicule, correcting by this means the manifest errors of popular belief.

Each adventure ends in a similar way with the hero of one and the heroine of the other settling down to a life of cozy domesticity and cultivating their respective gardens, the Eden-like qualities of which serve similar allegorical functions. Not even Shaw dared contradict or distort the harmonious resolution Voltaire brought to his tale, and he abided by it when taking his adventure beyond *Candide* to the arrival of the Irishman and everything that followed from this.

So, then, the two books are unalike and alike, superficially different but with pronounced overarching affinities, with *The Black Girl* complementing and developing its forerunner even when Shaw appears to be veering away from it.

I should cite another—postpublication—similarity, and it is that both books, when published in 1759 and 1932, had to endure parallel rites of passage. *Candide* outraged religious and political authority; it was condemned, confiscated, and burned; yet it became a best-seller throughout Europe. *The Black Girl* ran the same gauntlet of outrage; it was also condemned, confiscated, and, in at least one case, burned; and it too became a best-seller.

There are no other obvious precursors of *The Black Girl* following *Candide* until one comes to the nearly contemporary play *Liluli* by the French writer Romain Rolland.[5] Shaw and Rolland were acquainted but not enthusiastic about each other, for reasons that are extraneous to this narrative. Nevertheless, Rolland sent Shaw a copy of *Liluli* in 1918; Shaw responded fulsomely—it is colossal, grand, very beautiful, magnificent—and thanks largely to his efforts, *Liluli* was performed in England.

How this was done strains the imagination, for it is very poor as a play. What there is as a plot squats in its overweight rural setting and refuses to budge; a cast of hundreds representing a diversity of allegorical figures—some recognizably from commedia dell'arte—wanders on, has its say, and wanders off. A one-character "chorus," a humpbacked doggish dolt named Polichinello ("Punch" in English), whom Michel Pharand sees as the play's Everyman,[6] provides continuous, usually sardonic, commentary, while a spritelike creature, Liluli, representing "illusion," hovers and hides, enticing ill-fated romantics and idealists to their doom. Pharand comments, "in keeping with the frenzy of war which [the play] mocks, it is fraught with fast-paced confusion."[7] The play as a play is fraught with slow-paced confusion. There is no influence on *The Black Girl* here, except that the many characters that cross the stage in *Liluli* are on a quest to discover . . . what? Escape from the intolerable burden of life, the mountain peak, a carefree future, the Promised Land?—even though, as Polichinello remarks, "the Promised Land . . . is always for tomorrow."[8]

But see *Liluli* in another way—as a procession or, better, as a cavalcade or pageant (with minipageants occurring in the action) in which such figures as a mute "opinion," "armed Peace," "diplomats," "intellectuals," and other members of the body politic strut their minute upon the stage and depict the insensate lusts of war in different guises (and express themselves in murderous rationalizations)—see it as a pageant with a series of set pieces, then one must allow that it had impact enough to merit a degree of Shaw's praise. As a satirical attack on the total war machine, on all the forces—military, civil, economic, intellectual, and psychological—that combine and conspire to create and perpetuate war, it wields powerful blows, more so for being delivered in a spirit of bitter raillery. Shaw and Rolland were of a mind in this. But there is not much of *The Black Girl* here. One asks, Where then?

The answer may be in a few of the allegorical figures, in what they say and do and wear, and the principal figure among these is "Master-God." It is tempting to discuss him at length because he is a splendidly cunning creation, particularly when he decks himself out in a white dressing gown with a golden sun in front and a moon on the back and delivers an ironic elegy on the demise of Jehovah and the eternal verities he once represented. But he anticipates Shaw's two early "Jehovahs"—the first who demanded burned flesh and the second who nailed Job in argument—in only the broadest of terms. If there is a link, it is in that these three "gods" are all masters of high-sounding mendacity.

There is another possible link, extratextual and possibly more concrete than those inhering in the quest motif and the resemblance be-

tween Master-God and Shaw's gods. This is that Rolland's play as published contained woodcuts illustrating the characters in boldly realized
relief. That depicting Master-God in his embroidered dressing gown is a
good example. His head is surrounded by a halo provided by a radiant
sun, and his features are emblematic of cunning and cynicism; Polichinello makes humble obeisance on one side, and Truth in her Harlequin
outfit stands aloof on the other. The illustrations have none of the fine
artistry that John Farleigh would provide for *The Black Girl,* but the images were there in Rolland's text for Shaw to examine. Perhaps something about them could have impressed itself on his mind to make him
amenable to his printer William Maxwell's suggestion a decade later to
embellish his text with woodcuts.

Rolland was no Voltaire, and I return now to Voltaire as a fictional
character in the Black Girl's quest. His is obviously a summating role, as
is made clear when the Black Girl, having rejected all the false gods she
has encountered in the forest, observes an old gentleman outside a prim
little villa working in his garden. This is Voltaire. She joins him in the
garden and is soon listening to him while he expounds his version of God,
or rather a Shavian version of Voltairean Deism. Not long afterward, a
red-haired Irishman arrives on the scene to till the kitchen garden and
"modernize" Voltaire's Deism by grafting Creative Evolution to it. That
concludes the allegory. The Black Girl has not found God but contentedly
adopts, for the time being at least, the dicta her two mentors have inculcated in her.

For the time being: there is a future beyond the pages of the book,
when the old gentleman will have died, the Black Girl's children have
grown up, and her husband, the Irishman, has become an unconscious
habit of hers. For Shaw, who never wasted a word, least of all in as tightly
knit a tale as this, leaves his allegory open-ended and ambiguous. In the
last sentences, one sees his Black Girl, her mind strengthened, thrown
back on the question that had induced her search: "Where is God?" By
now she will have learned that he lies beyond the smashing of idols with
a knobkerry, beyond even the prim little villa and its garden, and on as far
as thought can reach.

I will examine the theological difference between Deism and Creative
Evolution more closely in chapter 7. The important issue here is that
Shaw represents Voltaire as the best of human beings in an imperfect
world, infinitely superior to the gods who have attempted to seduce the

Black Girl with false argument. He accords Voltaire the ultimate salute and declares in effect that Voltaire has achieved a significance in Shaw's career that exceeds that of any other figure in the Western canon. If it is "antecedent" one is looking for, this eighteenth-century exemplar of "pure intelligence" stands head and shoulders above everyone else.

One wonders if Shaw would have written *The Black Girl* had Voltaire not predated him and pointed the way. The answer is quite possibly no. Their consanguinity has to be considered.

Voltaire is in many ways the model for Shaw's world-bettering crusades. Though separated by different nationalities, languages, and nearly two hundred years of history, they seem like two sides of the same coin within the Western tradition, the Voltairean "Ecrasez l'infame" of the eighteenth century translated and given an Irish lilt in the twentieth: "Crush the evil!" Many and frequent were the occasions and the opportunities for this cry then as now, as both careers testify. The following appreciation of Voltaire and the parallels that emerge are striking:

> That is the spectacle which, from *Les Délices* and Ferney, for twenty-three years, Voltaire displayed to a Europe alternately enthusiastic and scandalized, but always amused. For twenty-three years he succeeded in this miracle, of being the news of the day, of providing the last word, comic or serious but always unexpected, which filled the public ear.... For twenty-three years, Voltaire's was the noisiest toy trumpet in Europe.
>
> No doubt noise was agreeable to him and popular applause necessary. He never worried if there was a little contempt in the laughter of the gallery; he had never donned the stiff armor of moralism, the shell of dignity which makes the vainest and most ambitious of men preserve the postures of decorum. Having the glories of wit and beneficence, he did not disdain those won by contortion and grimaces. But in all his harlequinades he had his idea, which never quitted him any more than his self-esteem. He wanted to improve the social order. After 1755, and above all from 1760 to his death, one may say he never wrote a single page which did not criticize an abuse or propose a reform.... One must be blind with prejudice not to sense the profound and disinterested conviction which lies behind his principal attitudes....
>
> In reality, dearly as he prized the arts of literature and poetry, they

became nothing more to him than a means to an end. Tragedies and verses served to hasten the spread of his ideas. . . .

He has all the qualities, with many of the faults, of the journalist, above all the gift of the immediate, and the penetrating voice which carries and fixes our attention through the noisy confusion of life.[9]

This could be applied to Shaw in almost every particular. A Europe, later—in Shaw's case—a world, enthusiastic, scandalized, always amused. Being the news of the day, providing the last word, comic or serious but always unexpected, not for twenty-three years but for nearly half a century. The noisiest toy trumpet of the age. (One of the responses of the several that were brought out after publication of *The Black Girl* features Shaw banging a drum.) His need of popular applause, his refusal to don the "stiff armor of moralism," the "glories of wit and beneficence," above all, his mission to improve the world. There is no need to continue, except to point out that the world, still determinedly unimproved, has tended to forget the colossus that Shaw became in the first fifty years of the century. He was the Voltaire of the age, including in his allegiance to journalism, and although he refrained from advertising it himself, it seems that he wished to be regarded as such by his contemporaries and, in all likelihood, posterity.

He was also a practiced name-dropper. Those years in the reading room of the British Museum were not confined to Karl Marx and economics; Voltaire would have been part of the Shavian curriculum, and his name, when dropped into letters, prefaces, plays, and other constituents of Shaw's writings, is done with assurance and almost always approvingly, as though putting Voltaire forward as the very model of high Shavian intelligence sensibly applied. The résumé that follows highlights the Voltairean presence in a selection of Shaw's principal writings.

One of the earliest occasions is in a music review of 1891, where Shaw (dropping three names) remarks that "Every schoolboy . . . remembers Macaulay's story of how Voltaire received Congreve's snobbish application to be regarded as a gentleman, and not as a writer for the theatre. 'If you were merely a gentleman,' said Voltaire, 'I should not have bothered to come and see you.'"[10]

This is anecdote, not worth much in itself, although it throws some light on Shaw's approval of Voltaire's opinion of the "gentleman." However, at this time (1891) Voltaire is incorporated in a Shavian text in a far more substantial way, in the chapter in *The Quintessence of Ibsenism* titled "The Two Pioneers." Shaw is discussing the "crablike progress of social evolution, which the individual advances by seeming to go backward, continues to illude us." But in the end the "pious man is at last forced to admit . . . that the disciples of Voltaire and Tom Paine do not pick pockets or cut throats oftener than your even Christian: he is actually driven to doubt whether Voltaire himself (poor Voltaire, who built a church, and was the greatest philanthropist of his time!) really screamed and saw the devil on his deathbed."

Shaw then points out that, in time, even the rationalist will fall into the same conservatism, and the Voltairean freethinker will go his way even as his predecessor, the exemplar of the age of faith, had to go. He continues:

> One of the first and most famous utterances of rationalism would have condemned it without further hearing had its full significance been seen at the time. Voltaire, taking exception to the trash of some poetaster, was met with the plea, "One must live." "I don't see the necessity," replied Voltaire. The evasion was worthy of the Father of Lies himself; for Voltaire was face to face with the very necessity he was denying; must have known, consciously or not, that it is the universal postulate; would have understood, if he had lived today, that since all valid human institutions are constructed to fulfil man's will, and his will is to live even when his reason teaches him to die, logical necessity, which was the sort Voltaire meant . . . can never be a motor in human actions, and is, in short, not necessity at all.

Later: "The deists, Voltaire and Tom Paine, were, to the divines of their day, predestined devils, tempting mankind hellward." This has a 1912 footnote: "This is not precisely true. Voltaire was what we should now call an advanced Congregationalist: in fact, modern Dissent, on its educated side, is sound Voltaireanism."[11]

Shaw here—and in a comparatively early stage of his public career—has plainly adopted Voltaire as a major ally in his campaigns, even when finding a shortcoming in his failure to recognize the limitations of logical necessity. One wonders whether he is not making unduly heavy philosophical weather of the matter, especially as Voltaire was probably indulging in a flippant put-down of a literary nonentity. At the same time, one may see this as pointing to the very issue on which Shaw parted company with Voltaire in *The Black Girl*, on which his Creative Evolution branched away from the "logical necessity" of Voltairean Deism.

This particular matter did not end here. His friend and the most dedicated of his many critics, William Archer, reviewed *The Quintessence* in the November 1891 issue of the *New Review* as an "Open Letter to George Bernard Shaw," and Shaw responded typically with a rebuttal: "What you say of the Voltaire point is hopelessly fudged by your overlooking my careful limitation of the meaning of his 'necessity' to logical necessity. The whole gist of my criticism of him is that he did regard lack of logical necessity as lack of real necessity."[12]

Voltaire reappears some ten years later, in 1903, in the "Epistle Dedicatory to Arthur Bingham Walkley"—the preface to *Man and Superman*—where he is invoked in passing but in terms that indicate that he now has a permanent place in the Shavian reference library, even while Shaw appears to be repudiating him. "I do not know"—Shaw remarks to Walkley—"whether you have any illusions left on the subject of education, progress, and so forth. I have none. Any pamphleteer can shew the way to better things; but when there is no will there is no way." Later, returning to this theme, he inveighs against Voltaire's "theistic credulity": "In vain do I redouble the violence of the language in which I proclaim my heterodoxies. I rail at the theistic credulity of Voltaire, the amoristic superstition of Shelley, the revival of tribal soothsaying and idolatrous rites which Huxley called Science. . . . And yet, instead of exclaiming, "Send this inconceivable Satanist to the stake," the respectable newspapers pith me by announcing "another book by this brilliant and thoughtful writer."[13]

Two things may be said about this. The first is that Shaw in the early 1900s was by no means a favorite of the "respectable newspapers," who would happily have sent the "inconceivable Satanist" to the stake had they thought him important enough and anyway much preferred the lazy option, which was to ignore him. The second point is that perhaps without consciously realizing it, Shaw is casting himself in a similar role to that adopted by Voltaire in his antiestablishment campaigns.

Voltaire then makes a brief and abrupt appearance in 1904 in *The Commonsense of Municipal Trading*, where Shaw presents him as an authority on tax and rentals, even citing his *Homme aux Quarante Écus* (a title that recurs in *Great Catherine* and again in *Everybody's Political*

What's What?) as adding muscle to the Shavian thesis. After this, by way
of light relief, in a 1905 letter to Vladimir Tchertkoff, he intimates that
anyone who so much as hinted at Shakespeare's "philosophic deficiencies" would be metaphorically clasped to the Shavian bosom with hoops
of steel: "Of course you know about Voltaire's criticisms, which are the
more noteworthy because Voltaire began with an extravagant admiration for Shakespeare, and got more and more bitter against him as he
grew older, and less disposed to accept artistic merit as a cover for philosophic deficiencies."[14]

There is a more substantial tribute in the "Preface for Politicians"—
the preface to *John Bull's Other Island* (1907)—where Voltaire may now
be seen to be firmly established in the Shavian pantheon. He is featured
in a subheading, "English Voltaireanism," then set up, by strong implication, as an eighteenth-century Shavian:

> [The Englishman] thinks of Voltaire as a French "infidel," instead of
> as the champion of the laity against the official theocracy of the
> State Church. The Nonconformist leaders of our Free Churches are
> all Voltaireans. The warcry of the Passive Resister is Voltaire's
> warcry, "Ecrasez l'infame".... Voltaire convinced the Genevan min-
> isters that he was the philosophic champion of their Protestant, In-
> dividualistic, Democratic Deism against the State Church of Roman
> Catholic France; and his heroic energy and beneficence as a philan-
> thropist, which now only makes the list of achievements on his
> monument at Ferney the most impressive epitaph in Europe. . . .
> Unfortunately [he] had an irrepressible sense of humor. He joked
> about Habakkuk. . . . And so [he] . . . became in England the bogey-
> atheist of three generations of English ignoramuses, instead of the
> legitimate successor of Martin Luther and John Knox.[15]

The reference to Voltaire in the preface to *Major Barbara* (1907) takes
one back to the admission in the "Epistle Dedicatory" to Walkley that
Shaw had no illusions left regarding the efficacy of the printed word:
"It has been said that the French Revolution was the work of Voltaire,
Rousseau and the Encyclopedists. It seems to me to have been the work of
men who had observed that virtuous indignation, caustic criticism, con-
clusive argument and instructive pamphleteering, even when done by
the most earnest and witty literary geniuses, were as useless as praying,
things going steadily from bad to worse whilst the Social Contract and

the pamphlets of Voltaire were at the height of their vogue . . . I, who have preached and pamphleteered like any Encyclopedist, have to confess that my methods are no use, and would be no use if I were Voltaire, Rousseau, Bentham, Marx, Mill, Dickens, Carlyle, Ruskin, Butler and Morris all rolled into one."[16] That Shaw is identifying himself with his eighteenth- and nineteenth-century forerunners—that he recognizes his kinship with the brotherhood of preachers and pamphleteers mentioned in this passage, with Voltaire in particular—is obvious.

A passing amusing reference to him in an exchange between Tanner and Straker in *Man and Superman* is followed in the "Preface on Doctors"—the preface to *The Doctor's Dilemma* (1911)—by a disparaging remark to the effect that Voltaire, Catherine II of Russia, and Lady Mary Wortley Montagu expected smallpox to be made harmless by the old practice of inoculation. This is one of Shaw's few sideswipes at Voltaire (and Voltaire two hundred years ago was possibly more right in the matter of smallpox inoculation than Shaw allowed himself to be, crankily questioning the efficacy of vaccination as he did throughout his adult life). Immediately afterward, in the preface to *Getting Married* (1911), he makes amends by citing him as an authority on a basic principle of government: "The voter's duty is to take care that the Government consists of men whom he can trust to devize or support institutions making for the common welfare. This is highly skilled work; and to be governed by people who set about it as the man in the street would set about it is to make straight for 'red ruin and the breaking up of laws.' Voltaire said that Mr. Everybody is wiser than anybody; and whether he is or not, it is his will that must prevail."[17]

There is this in "Parents and Children," the preface to *Misalliance* (1910): "And when a man arises with a soul of sufficient native strength to break the bonds of this inculcated reverence and to expose and deride and tweak the noses of our humbugs and panjandrums, like Voltaire and Dickens, we are shocked and scandalized, even when we cannot help laughing."[18] Did Shaw have to resist the temptation to include his name with Voltaire and Dickens? Certainly the conflation of "shocked and scandalized" with "laughing" points to him as much as it does to these predecessors.

Then in the four-scene play *Great Catherine* (first performed in 1913), Voltaire features as a major point of reference offstage. I quote at length, the better to show how Shaw incorporates and establishes Voltaire's intellectual preeminence within the conventions of farce:

> THE SERGEANT . . . Little Father: the English captain, so highly recommended to you by old Fritz of Prussia, by the English ambassador, and by Monsieur Voltaire (whom [*crossing himself*] may God in his infinite mercy damn eternally!), is in the antechamber and desires audience.
>
> PATIOMKIN [*deliberately*] To hell with the English captain; and to hell with old Fritz of Prussia; and to hell with Monsieur Voltaire; and to hell with you too![19]

Later, when one meets the English captain, Edstaston, one may wonder why Voltaire should have thought fit to recommend him to Catherine: surely he knew, sly fox that he was, that the empress would enjoy turning him inside out, stuffy opinionated duffer that Edstaston is. One encounters this passage soon after the great Catherine comes on stage:

> THE PRINCESS DASHKOFF. God knows, Little Mother, we all implore you to give your wonderful brain a rest. That is why you get headaches. Monsieur Voltaire also has headaches. His brain is just like yours.
>
> CATHERINE. Dashkoff: what a liar you are! . . . Let me tell you I would not give a rouble to have the brains of all the philosophers in France.[20]

Is this a jocular indication of Shaw identifying himself with Voltaire, for as every Shavian knows, another "wonderful brain," Shaw's own, was similarly prone to periodic blinding headaches? As an "in-house" joke, this would have tickled Shaw's fancy, possibly also that of members of the cast who knew him well, such as Gertrude Kingston, for whom Shaw wrote the part of Catherine. Also, notwithstanding the seeming casualness of Catherine's dismissal of all the philosophers in France, one discerns the comment on the relative significance of the "Doer," which the empress assuredly was, and the "Thinker," which is what Voltaire represents, when it comes to ruling a country.

Voltaire is a major presence in the climax of the play, the linchpin of the action as Catherine extols his virtues and Edstaston, the typical Englishman that Shaw loved to lampoon—bigoted, blinkered, and yet not unintelligent or lacking in courage—staunchly resists her "torture," at least initially. However, delivered bound to the empress and admitting to being "ticklesome," he is quite at her mercy.

> *Catherine and Edstaston are now alone. Catherine has in her hand a sceptre or baton of gold. Wrapped round it is a new pamphlet, in French, entitled L'Homme aux Quarante Écus. She calmly unrolls this and begins to read it at her ease as if she were quite alone. Several seconds elapse in dead silence. She becomes more and more absorbed in the pamphlet, and more and more amused by it.*
>
> CATHERINE [*greatly pleased by a passage, and turning over the leaf*] Ausgezeichnet!
> EDSTASTON. Ahem!
> *Silence. Catherine reads on.*
> CATHERINE. Wie komisch!
> EDSTASTON. Ahem! ahem!
> *Silence*
> CATHERINE [*soliloquizing enthusiastically*] What a wonderful author is Monsieur Voltaire! How lucidly he exposes the folly of this crazy plan for raising the revenue of the country from a single tax on land! how he withers it with his irony! how he makes you laugh whilst he is convincing you! how sure one feels that the proposal is killed by his wit and economic penetration: killed never to be mentioned again among educated people!
> EDSTASTON. For Heaven's sake, Madam, do you intend to leave me tied up like this while you discuss the blasphemies of that abominable infidel? Agh! [*She has again applied her toe*]. Oh! Oo!
> CATHERINE [*calmly*] Do I understand you to say Monsieur Voltaire is a great philanthropist and a great philosopher as well as the wittiest man in Europe?
> EDSTASTON. Certainly not. I say that his books ought to be burnt by the common hangman [*her toe touches his ribs*]. Yagh! Oh don't. I shall faint. I cant bear it.
> CATHERINE. Have you changed your opinion of Monsieur Voltaire?
> EDSTASTON. But you cant expect me as a member of the Church of England [*she tickles him*] B Agh! Ow! Oh Lord! he is anything you like. He is a philanthropist, a philosopher, a beauty: he ought to

have a statue, damn him! [*she tickles him*] No! bless him! Save him victorious, happy and glorious! Oh, let eternal honors crown his name: Voltaire thrice worthy on the rolls of fame! [*Exhausted*]. Now will you let me up? And look here! I can see your ankles when you tickle me: it's not ladylike.[21]

Given the "ticklesome" situation presented here, one may be inclined to ask if the scene (the play as a whole for that matter) is no more than a frothy *pièce d'occasion*. The answer is no, far from it. One may press a three-pronged point regarding the "serious" undertone: it is historical fact that Catherine was a great admirer of Voltaire; Voltaire's demolition of the idea of a land tax strikes a contemporary chord in that it endorses Fabian opposition to such a policy; and, third, Catherine emerges here as Shaw's mouthpiece, arguing a case for Shaw himself, a latter-day Voltaire who was denounced in his day for his heresies as Voltaire was in his day.

There is no need to pursue Shaw's Voltaireanism in detail beyond this point. *Great Catherine* marks an apogee, at least in the early and middle period. "The Infidel Half Century," the preface to *Back to Methuselah* (1918–21), contains several allusions to Voltaire, while the fifth play of the Pentateuch, *As Far As Thought Can Reach*, has an amusing (and, some may think, a blasphemous) reference by Pygmalion to surviving fragments of pictures and documents that represent a "very remarkable early experimenter . . . the founder of biological science . . . walking in a garden and advising people to cultivate their gardens. "His name"— Pygmalion says—"has come down to us in several forms. One of them is Jove. Another is Voltaire."[22] This is not a flippant witticism but rather the suggestion that Voltaire's name has survived the desuetude of the ages and remains a "presence even here in the illimitable future. In the preface to *Saint Joan* (1923), Shaw defends Voltaire's treatment of Joan in his poem *La Pucelle*, where the purpose had been not to present a "fair" portrait of Joan but "to kill with ridicule everything that Voltaire righteously hated in the institutions and the fashions of his own day."[23]

One moves on, and back, to the crux of this discussion, to 1932, to that moment in her search for God when the Black Girl, having been disappointed in all her previous encounters, happens upon "a prim little villa with a "very amateurish garden" being cultivated by "a wizened old gentleman whose . . . face was all intelligence."[24] This is Voltaire, of course.

As all these references and allusions make clear, Voltaire was Shaw's lodestar in many ways, an abiding but never ostentatious presence throughout the intellectual odyssey of his life. His appearance and the role he plays in the Black Girl's search are no sudden arbitrary events but the logical outcome of this companionship, the reiteration of what the previous forty years have emphasized, that Shaw regarded Voltaire as the brightest luminary of modern Western history, representing in himself the emancipated intellect squaring up to and battling the forces of institutional reactionism and corruption. More than this, Shaw equated his career with Voltaire's, seeing himself in a special relationship with his predecessor and identifying himself spiritually and intellectually with all that he stood for.

There has been surprisingly little critical work on the topic pursued here—the Shaw-Voltaire connection. Shaw's French translator, Augustin Hamon, insisting in his critical-eulogistic essays on the Shaw-Molière affinity, or what he saw as an affinity, scarcely paused to consider Voltaire; while American scholars have considered the topic, often with insight, but comparatively briefly. Recently, however, Michel W. Pharand, in the chapter "Optimistic Vitalism" in his *Bernard Shaw and the French*, compares and contrasts mainly the religious attitudes of each, taking the topic leagues beyond previous rather casual appreciations.

There is also *The Adventures of God in His Search for the Black Girl* by the British novelist Brigid Brophy. Coming to this, one comes to fantasy. Derived from Shaw's allegory and Shavian to the nth degree, it is an original in its own right and may be considered here because Brophy— seeing the kinship between Voltaire and Shaw more clearly than any predecessor had done—brings them together in an afterlife (with one or two other historical "greats," not to mention God himself), where they get together and discuss a wide range of topics, principally the question of God's "reality."

The Adventures of God is audaciously and exuberantly a sequel to Shaw's tale, a taking of the quest beyond the Voltairean garden to the Elysian Fields, from where God himself sets out to look for the Black Girl. Quite why he should want to find her is not clear at first, because he is easily distracted from his mission, and, discovering Gibbon and Voltaire disputing the nature of faith with a psychoanalyst, a historian, a theologian, and a humble Christian, he allows himself to be drawn into the discussion. It is with some hesitation that he involves himself, however.

As he puts it, he felt diffident about joining in because the others were all historical characters whereas he is a fictitious one. As such, he has his own validity; even so, there were certain anomalies peculiar to his situation that disquieted him and made him unsure of himself—the main anomaly being that his creators had put it about that *he* had created *them*.[25]

God's problems are compounded by the way believers have portrayed him, attributing all calamities, disasters, and accidents, all arbitrary violence, suffering, sickness, and ugliness to him and his "mysterious ways." Not surprisingly, he has become the "most hateful character in fiction" with a reputation damaged beyond repair. This is why, as the reader gradually learns, he has set out to find the Black Girl: he wants her to refurbish his image.

This will not happen for some time yet, as Brophy, launching herself into her Socratic-Shavian dialogue, has God discussing with the others, principally Voltaire, such issues as "the English and their two major passions—their sense of propriety and their sense of property" (140–1), vegetarianism, feminism, vivisection, the state of Ireland, established religions, the crime of poverty, and other Shavian issues. God also has a couple of set-tos with the humble Christian, who insists most unhumbly and dogmatically that the Bible is the Word of God, and that God should venerate it as such.

Realizing that God is under some misapprehension about the Black Girl, Voltaire takes it on himself to be his guide when he resumes his quest. And it is thanks to Voltaire (following a farcical episode in which God hoists up his robe and chases after a tall "Black Woman who turns out to be, not the Black Girl, but a representative of "Hallelujah Hall") that he finally reaches his destination, the cultivated garden. There is no Black Girl here, only "a tallish, bony-hipped figure wearing narrow trousers and something resembling a norfolk jacket" (182–3). It is Shaw, who wastes little time in launching into a withering attack on "the Irish" in which Brophy is at her Shavian best in her take-off of her subject, the gist of which is that the national pastime of the Irish is suttee combined with the Irishman's unselfish devotion to cutting off his own and everyone else's nose to spite his face (184–6).

God's misapprehension about the Black Girl is brought home to him. He shamefacedly explains that he had mistaken her *Adventures* for an autobiographical story, and that he had hoped, since in the book she was so anxious to meet him, that if she did meet him she might undertake a sequel and tell people what he was truly like (187).

Voltaire tells Shaw he has already brought together a "few people who are willing to bend their talents towards promoting a more just appreciation of God." Would Shaw—? "A celestial Fabian Society?" Shaw enquires. "I will join it" (187).

So the three go off together—Shaw followed (as in his mortal existence he had said he would be) by a menagerie of domesticated beasts representing the grateful animals he did not eat in his lifetime—and join Gibbon and the psychoanalyst at a handsome round table that God spontaneously creates, "exerting the power of fiction" in doing so. Here, amid the interjections and irrelevancies that characterize the tale, the committee produces (in Shaw's shorthand) the declaration:

TO WHOM IT MAY CONCERN
I do not exist
Signed, with divine authority,
GOD

There is an epilogue. In it a goose (a dove apparently not being available) distributes this declaration over St. Peter's Square in Rome, where the leaflets fall upon an assortment of markedly unattractive "pilgrims" who, to a man (and woman), are as impervious to messages from on high as they are self-engrossed.

The meeting of Shaw and Voltaire could, one feels, have generated historic talk, and there are some exchanges that hint at "significance." These begin in the garden, where Voltaire tells Shaw that he had taken a look at the manner in which Shaw had furnished his home, which was an abiding monument to his total visual insensibility" (183). Then, still in the garden after God has explained his mistake about the Black Girl, Shaw tells them that she had been sketched from literature. "I couldn't give her a name, because I had already used the name Candida elsewhere. But she is simply a black and female version of Voltaire's hero Candide." Voltaire is flattered but reminds Shaw that it is God's rehabilitation they have to consider. "After all, one of the most notable rehabilitations in history was officially accorded to Saint Joan, and there you are even more of an expert than I" (187).

There are one or two passing remarks between the two (Shaw says for example that Voltaire was one of those from whom he had learned that effectiveness of assertion was the alpha and omega of style), but it is only in the course of a lengthy "irrelevancy," a discussion of the question of "character" in novels and plays, that they speak directly to each other and at length. They agree that "character" as such does not exist. As Shaw puts it, he had begun his career as a dramatist by lifting his characters out of pages of Dickens and discovered that he had thereby produced an effect of daring innovation and originality. Voltaire agrees that Shaw had actually been a daring innovator and original, to which the psychoanalyst contributes his view that "character is indeed *so* insubstantial." The very characters who, in Dickens, were recognized as "human," were accused, when they reappeared in the pages or on the stages of Shaw, of being dehumanized, intellectualized and mere mouthpieces for ideas. "It is an inexplicable paradox," Shaw says, "that people regularly regard ideas as dehumanized. . . . Yet the truth is that ideas are the *most* human of [attributes]" (202).

Voltaire remarks later that "Shaw liked to give his outcomes [of his plays] an exact ironic point (though, if I may, as a fellow dramatist, make a technical observation, he was very bad at curtain lines)" (203). This leads to his turning a neat but intricate compliment about Shaw's plays: "You were afraid of psychology . . . because of what you termed your delicacy. And it was the same thing that made you afraid of art. Even the most intellectual elements in art, namely design and the ideas, are sensuous: if the artist gets them right, their rightness is a matter of pleasure, not external logic. You were so deep a puritan that you could not admit you wrote for art's sake but had to pretend it was for Lamarckianism's sake. However, for art's sake I can't be sorry, since the products of your pretence were works of art" (204–5).

Voltaire soon balances this with an unequivocal put-down of *Saint Joan*, after Shaw has warned God that, if he wishes his "godifesto" to include an epilogue, he should forearm himself against the advice of well-meaning persons to eliminate it. Voltaire's advice is to "keep the epilogue and cut out the play," Shaw's only wholly bad one, he says, "which is no doubt why it is your most famous one." It is, he tells Shaw, nothing but a succession of static tableaux illustrating medieval life and would pass for a village pageant whose producer was severely under the influence of the pre-Raphaelites. Joan was such a plaster pre-Raphaelite saint that all right-thinking people declared that Shaw had given up joking and written a great play at last. They meant that he had temporarily given up disturbing them. "You came back to your sense only with the Epilogue" (205–7).

Shaw's response to this is mildness itself. He does not, on the whole, dispute Voltaire's verdict regarding *Saint Joan,* but he would wager that his best play, *Heartbreak House,* would not be produced or prescribed reading at schools.

This concludes the Voltaire-Shaw exchanges. It goes without saying that the opinions, literary and otherwise, that Brophy ascribes to the choice and master spirits of her cast are her own, but to the extent that one can attribute authority of voice to the roles, Voltaire is the leading man with Shaw a shaky second, partly because he appears rather late in the action. God is always "on stage," but his is an apologetic, rather defensive voice. Voltaire knows Shaw's work well (though not, it seems, his "Voltairean" crusades) and treats him and his plays with respect while feeling free, no doubt as the senior of the two, to criticize him when necessary. Apart from the pro-Voltairean remark in the preface to *Saint Joan*—which he mentions—he does not seem aware of all the other occasions Shaw brought him into his discourses. This is to say that Brophy has not delved into Shaw's work as deeply as she should.

Oddly, she does not mention the crucial role Voltaire plays in *The Black Girl.* Neither the Black Girl nor the wizened old gentleman is in the garden, which is understandable considering that both are "fictions" and therefore not present in the larger "reality" of Brophy's fiction. Even so, the "real" Voltaire of Brophy's fiction would surely have known of the "fictional" one in *The Black Girl.* He does not seem to; or at all events he does not acknowledge Shaw's tribute to him in the book. Brophy glosses over this and other minor complications, which is perhaps just as well: *The Adventures of God* is much too buoyantly high-spirited to be weighed down by complexities of this kind.

One other Voltaire-Shaw reference may be cited: a letter Shaw wrote in 1928 to a certain unrelated Mabel Shaw, a missionary in Northern Rhodesia (Zambia). More will be said in chapter 2 about their association and Mabel Shaw's "responsibility" for *The Black Girl.* It is necessary here to quote an excerpt that deals with Voltaire:

> [W]e all have our superstitions and our complexes, the difference between a mad writer like Saint Paul and a rather sane one like Voltaire being only one of degree. One can only say it would have

been better for the world if Paul had never been born, and that it would have been a great misfortune—a religious misfortune—to have missed Voltaire, who at least loved justice and did mercy and walked humbly with his God, and believed that no further theology was required of him. Also he certainly loved mercy and, as far as his temperament would let him, tried to do justly. That is why he is still so readable. Besides, as the wickednesses which he exposed and which he called on the world's conscience to renounce were too frightful to be contemplated without some sort of anaesthetic, he used his sense of fun to make people come to scoff, knowing that was the only chance of getting them to remain to pray.[26]

It is no wonder the Black Girl laid down her knobkerry and, opening the gate, entered the old gentleman's garden.

2

Foreshadowing

The story behind the story of the Black Girl begins with the person Shaw wrote to in praise of Voltaire—the missionary Mabel Shaw. Unlikely as it may seem, their correspondence in the late 1920s and early 1930s prefigured *The Black Girl* in a profound way, as Shaw would come to acknowledge.

He learned about her from an acquaintance, J. E. Whiting, a Quaker and chairman of the Arthington Trust, which disbursed money to various missionary organizations, among them the London Missionary Society. Shaw donated money to the Trust—"I can hardly refuse an infinitesimal percentage of the money I have made out of [Joan]."[1] It was on the basis of this demonstration of goodwill that Whiting wrote to Shaw two months later about Mabel Shaw, who had been serving the London Missionary Society in Mbereshi, Northern Rhodesia (Zambia), since 1915. Mabel Shaw had written to Whiting's wife relating the story of her life, or, as Whiting expressed it to Shaw, the "History of God's dealings with her." He enclosed in his letter extracts from Mabel Shaw's letters to the London Missionary Society.[2] Shaw responded:

> I have read the enclosed with great interest. I waive the point that the Shaws have considerable literary talent and are not behindhand as liars, taking it that you can answer for the lady's address being correct, and her activities real. She makes it clear that a negro girl is far less of a savage than an average post war flapper. But I feel pretty angry with her for putting up that cross. When will people learn to introduce Christ as a teacher and not as a figure from the Chamber of Horrors? When the negroes have learnt to worship The Crucified, they have got no further than their worship of their own black king because he buried people alive under the doorposts of his hut.

. . . Miss Shaw's letters ought to be printed. Many thanks for send-ing them to me.[3]

Whiting sent a copy of this letter to Mabel Shaw, who responded with a spirited defense of the cross as the symbol of "the only way of Life that takes us home to God." She added that she had seen a performance of *Saint Joan* when "at home," that is, on leave in England, "and I saw God. The man who wrote that can never have been an agnostic. There are bits in St Joan I turn to when I need to be near the heart of God."[4]

Whiting may well have shown this to Shaw because, when replying to another letter from Whiting, Shaw mentioned Mabel Shaw again: "Tell Miss Shaw to publish her life *now*. All that waiting about until she and all her generation are dead should not count if the book will help people."[5]

There seems to have been a hiatus after this, and six months later, early in 1928, Shaw wrote again, this time to Mabel Shaw herself, Whit-ing having evidently suggested to Shaw that he evaluate her writing skills and offer advice.[6] Shaw begins by confirming that Mabel Shaw wrote well and as far as mere literary faculty went was well qualified to "take up literature as a profession." He adds, "But success in literature depends on what you have to say as well as on how you say it." He men-tions Bunyan as having written *The Holy War* more skillfully than *The Pilgrim's Progress,* but the latter is the truly great work, while *The Holy War* makes theology ridiculous and unreadable.

Next comes the tribute to Voltaire, which in itself, if one considers the letter as presaging *The Black Girl,* is remarkable enough. Then:

Now it is clear from what you have written that you are one of the would-be saviors, like Bunyan and Voltaire. Having found happi-ness with God (so to speak) you wish to bring others to him. Jesus, who was strongly anti-missionary, as his warning about the tares and the wheat shews, would probably tell you to mind your own business and suffer little children to find their own way to God even if it were a black way; but he certainly would not demur to your describing your own pilgrimage and testifying that you had found God in your own white way. That is, if he had any patience with you after discovering that you had set up in the virgin forest the horrible emblem of Roman cruelty and Roman terrorism as an emblem of Christianity. Even Rome itself would have set up an image of a mother and child.

Shaw tells her that, in his opinion, her work would please a sufficient number of book buyers to make a profit for a publisher and bookseller and a living for her. He has found her "scraps" interesting, and he is not in sympathy with her at all. Then, most unexpectedly, he "lets rip," as though Mabel Shaw's action in becoming a missionary is a perversion of nature, a kind of self-torture:

> I am not in the least . . . a person with a queer lust for being tortured; so that when your parents no longer tortured you [Mabel Shaw's parents were apparently "detestable"] you tortured yourself. You are not satiated even with the horrible things they did to Christ: you must heap on him a broken body, though the story insists so strongly on the fact that his body was not broken as the bodies of the thieves were. You meet a young man with whom you fall in love, and who falls in love with you. There was nothing to prevent you making him and yourself happy by naturally and unaffectedly marrying him and filling your lap with babies. But no: that would not have been any fun for you: you must break his heart and break your own (if you have one) on the ridiculous pretext that the negro children needed you, though your own country was swarming with little white heathens who needed you. . . . And then comes your artistic impulse. You must write about it and make a propaganda of voluptuous agony. Well, there are plenty of people who find agony voluptuous on paper; and they will make a reading public for you. But I, who loathe torture, and object most strongly to being tortured, my lusts being altogether normal, should take you and shake you were it not that you are out of my reach and that you would rather enjoy being shaken if it hurt you enough.

Shaw softens this outburst in the next paragraph by suggesting that Mabel Shaw's "psychosis" would pass away as her glands mature; that there may be a young woman with a "healthy taste for travel, novelty, adventure, and salutary hardening hardship" at the bottom of the "African business"; that she may not really have wanted that unfortunate young parson whom she "smashed up"; that, being the granddaughter of a delightful old humbug of a grandmother who spoiled her and "saved her soul alive," there would come the time when she, Mabel Shaw, would be strong enough "to face adult life and grow out of the pastime of playing with the souls of little children as your soul was played with."

And that, he concludes, is all he has to say to her; but of course there is a Shavian coda: "I assure you the question of becoming a professional writer is a pretty deep one when the intention behind it extends to becoming a prophet as well. I am in that line myself; and I KNOW."

There are false assumptions here. Whiting, who seems to have been a gossipy soul, would have told Shaw about Mabel Shaw's "detestable parents," the "old humbug of a grandmother," and the young parson whose heart she was alleged to have broken. Shaw builds on this and assumes that she is a young woman when mentioning her "psychosis," her immature glands, and "healthy taste for travel." In fact, she was nearly forty—she was born in 1889 and died in 1973—and had been at the Mbereshi Mission since 1915. Also, as Dan Laurence points out, Shaw was apparently not aware that she was already a published author of two books and an educationist of note. Laurence cites Sean Morrow, who had undertaken a historical survey of the Mbereshi Mission, and who had told him that Mabel Shaw was a pioneer in her day "of a type of education for girls that sought to combine what she considered to be 'traditional' elements in African society with a Christian and English style of education."[7]

Mabel Shaw responded to Shaw's letter a year later. It had, she told him, roused much hot protest initially, but with the passage of time it gave her "more enjoyment as [she] read it, that deep quiet enjoyment that endures."[8] Some months afterward, in May 1930, Shaw entertained her to lunch at Whitehall Court. Charlotte was out of town and ill, and Nancy Astor stood in for her. Writing to Astor beforehand, Shaw described Mabel Shaw as "a woman with a craze for self torture, who broke off her engagement with a clergyman (he died of it) to bury herself in the wilds of Africa and lead negro children to Christ."[9] The stance remains critical, but it seems that, meeting her, Shaw—ever the courteous host—forbore from taking and shaking her, as once promised.

These false assumptions and the errors of judgment that followed from them scarcely matter when one considers the way Shaw's letter and entire association with Mabel Shaw foreshadow *The Black Girl*. The tribute to Voltaire and the references to Bunyan's works prefigure Shaw's allegory, as do his skepticism regarding Mabel Shaw's desire to bring black children to the white way of worshiping God and his loathing of the "horrible emblem of Roman cruelty"—the cross—that Mabel Shaw has set up in the "virgin forest," an image that is repeated in *The Black Girl*. Also repeated is the image of Christ on the cross, though here Shaw eschews the torture associated with the symbol in favor of the artist who facilely carves images of a crucified but uninjured (and quite chatty) "conjuror." Then, in sounding off about Mabel Shaw's refusal to marry the young clergyman, Shaw creates another image that went straight into *The Black Girl*, that of marrying and "naturally and unaffectedly . . . filling [her] lap with babies," which is what the Black Girl does after settling down in Voltaire's garden and villa and marrying the Irishman.

The tension in the letter—and there is considerable inner tension—emanates from a source other than Mabel Shaw herself; it originates in Shaw's aroused consciousness of the inherent problem of her mission, that of grafting a white, European-orientated religion on a black, African culture. He took this problem with him when he sailed for South Africa and included it as a major feature of his cogitations in the "interview" he drafted when still at sea; it was uppermost in his mind when he disembarked.

All in all, it is not difficult to see why Shaw would send Mabel Shaw a copy of *The Black Girl* when it was published, with the inscription, "I send you this story, for which you are really responsible, as it was you who set me thinking about the contact of black minds with white religions."[10] One need not guess at Mabel Shaw's reaction: it would certainly have been rejection of the book itself and of the compliment implicit in the inscription.

She is also a presence in the opening page and a bit of the book, as the "small white woman" missionary who converts the Black Girl. Something of the real person that Shaw had grown to know lingers in the miniature portrait, but it is the license afforded by fiction that vivifies it, making it magnified reality rather than verisimilitude, for one is being taken into the world of fantasy and exaggeration. His picture reflects to an uncanny degree the complacence of the public school system—very English, very select, very narrow: the upbringing that Mabel Shaw would foist on her black charges. He also brings in her aborted romance with the clergyman, who is turned into a succession of six brokenhearted suitors plus, spectacularly, the suicide of the last of the six.[11]

Shaw was greeted in Cape Town like a Roman returning in triumph. Members of the local branch of the Fabian Society, representatives from the Cape Town Publicity Bureau, admirers, the interested, the curious, the gapers and gawkers who are always somehow drawn to the famous as by a magnet—they all came on board and an audience of nearly one hundred surrounded him in the first-class lounge (Charlotte had fled to their cabin), where he gave an impromptu interview and affably posed and made a short speech before a "talkie" movie camera. One of his first questions to the Fabians—and it is an indication of the trend of his thinking even before landing—was whether "natives" were admitted to trade unions, the answer to which at the time was a qualified "no."

His arrival in Cape Town was "an event of national importance," as the evening newspaper, the *Cape Argus,* put it in a leader on the day of his arrival.[12] The prime minister, General J.B.M. Hertzog, endorsed this sentiment by writing him a letter of welcome. Both Hertzog and the paper, in their different ways, could not avoid slight spasms of anxiety at the thought of what Shaw might say about the country during his visit. As Hertzog engagingly put it: "I have been informed by our High Commissioner in London . . . that out of consideration for me and the many worries which presumably are troubling me, or should trouble me, you have decided not to do anything that will disturb the peace with me!"[13] And the *Cape Argus* leader read: "How will South Africa react to Mr. Shaw and he to us? No doubt our politics and our native policy will strike him as astonishingly funny. But, if our weather behaves nicely, our sun, and our respectful interest in Mr. Shaw, may lead him to deal lightly with our very obvious shortcomings."

In fact, Shaw and Hertzog got on extremely well when they met at a reception in his honor at the prime minister's official residence. But, in all conscience, how "lightly" could a man like Shaw deal with the "very obvious shortcomings" of the country when they were unrolled in daily display before his wondering eyes in the twelve weeks of his visit?

The morning paper, the *Cape Times,* was the lucky recipient of his first "interview," a self-drafted one like practically all of Shaw's considered statements for the press. This—a lengthy, thoughtful, and thought-provoking piece—was passed on to the paper within hours of his and Charlotte's arrival at their hotel and was printed the next morning.[14] If it had anything to declare, it was that Shaw, notwithstanding his avowal on board ship that he had had little time to give much thought to South Africa beforehand, had acquainted himself with the country sufficiently well to have quite a few anticipatory ideas on the situation that awaited him. His comments, though ranging over a diversity of Shavian subjects, were given a strong South African bias with, not surprisingly, the lack of social, economic, political, and legal status of the nonwhites in South African society a recurring topic. The Black Girl is a hidden presence here, although Shaw would not have realized it at this stage.

The interview begins with a comment on the question of the "black proletariat":

> It seems to me to create an appalling problem. The white man with a trade or profession or owning property is in a strong position, but when you have "poor whites" up against black men with a lower standard of living, what can you do with them? Simply drop them in the water?

Later, after a few remarks about the "breakdown of morality" since the war, he returned to the question of race and color, giving it a religious bias. The germ of *The Black Girl* may be discerned here; Mabel Shaw is a hovering shadow behind the comments: "The average modern Christian does not realize he is not a Christian, and does not know what it is to be a Christian. Yet he is making a Christian of the negroes. One does not know what is going to happen. Civilization is like a tree. It grows to a point and then perishes. We do not know that the next civilization may not be a black civilization. There is a danger in natives taking their Christianity with intense seriousness, because they will find out their teachers only profess to be Christians. The best thing would be to develop their intelligence and make them skeptics."

The absence in England of a religion concerned with human conduct and the presence of a "true religion" in Russia came next. One finds genuine religious fanaticism there, he said. The Russians have a religion, and it is that "all are equal—he may say before Marx." He continued: "No one believes here that the black man is the equal of the white, that the professional man is the equal of the retail shopkeeper, equal in the sight of God—but the Russians do believe it." These remarks tend to confirm the widespread view of Shaw as one of the most gullible of the celebrities who visited Russia in the 1930s. (He had visited it in 1931 and been enthusiastically received wherever he went, as was perhaps no less than his due as a man who had earned the attention of and a backhanded compliment from Lenin: "A good man fallen among Fabians"). Yet for all his mistaken reading of the reality underlying the Russian Revolution, he was in Cape Town and elsewhere throughout the 1930s enunciating the basic creed of his religious outlook, that all are equal in the sight of

God. This was a central tenet of Shavian belief, and it would be a major theme of *The Black Girl*.

A digression on trade came next. It was "a drawback on human existence," he said. "If you asked a business man what was his idea of a derelict place, he would say the Garden of Eden, because Eve gave Adam the apple instead of trading it." He returned to the subject of religion, commenting at length on the "tremendous moral force" that science was beginning to exert, that it was getting hold of men's souls and they were discovering that there was something outside themselves: "The moment science becomes religious, as it is becoming, men will find in it what they are seeking. If they go to ordinary religion they will find it is mixed up with things that no educated man can possibly believe. When they turn to science, religion will become scientific and politics will become scientific, as has happened to some extent in Russia." And it could happen, he may have wanted to add, to the black men and women of Africa.

When, in *The Black Girl*, the "scientists" comprising the Caravan of the Curious quiz the Black Girl and argue about the nature of the universe, it may seem that Shaw had changed his mind about "science" and its effect on men's lives. This is not so, as I will discuss in chapter 7.

The "interview" does not end until Shaw has expounded his belief in the Life Force—"some urge in men towards development"—and forcibly rejected the idea of personal immortality. "Think of me living forever—that the world could never get rid of me. No one could stand it. Think of your General Hertzog living for ever as an angel."

The printing of this unusually long and thorough interview is a measure of the importance South Africa attached to Shaw's visit. His was by no means an isolated "celebrity" visit—South Africa was a popular destination in those years for the notorious, the famous, and the titled (the Prince of Wales had visited the country in the late 1920s)—but his was among the most newsworthy, even when he and Charlotte tried to withdraw from public view to enjoy something of their intended private holiday. One might almost have believed Shaw when asked by the *Cape Argus* what his plans were: "Seeing South Africa and saying nothing," he replied. "Saying nothing?" People who knew him smiled. He had said a good deal on the day of his arrival, and he would say a good deal more before the visit was over, while newspaper reporters dogged his every footstep.

So it was that—apart from assorted "impromptus" on, among other things, the Cape Town Symphony Orchestra, the view from the top of Table Mountain (ascended by cable car), the expertise of a visiting escapologist, and his impressions of an airplane flight over the Cape Peninsula—he soon agreed to address the University of Cape Town Lunch Club (women graduates not admitted, to their loudly expressed chagrin), the Cape Town Breakfast Club, a public gathering in the city hall, the University of Stellenbosch, and—in a radio broadcast—the nation.

These addresses, the radio broadcast excepted, do not add anything to *The Black Girl* theme. It is as though Shaw decided to set aside the question of the "black proletariat" and their religious beliefs while attending to other South African issues: the idea of a university; the Anglo-Boer War; the miracle of modern Russia with its superheroes and Fabian-like permeation of "enemy" institutions; and the need, in view of South Africa's desperately inadequate agricultural resources, for the country to collect fertilizer from the atmosphere and adopt collective farming along Russian lines. The list could be extended, for Shaw was never short of issues and ideas. One such issue, an unwelcome one considering the sunny goodwill surrounding him, was foisted on him in the second week of the visit.

It was an attack on him by a visiting English Roman Catholic apologist, a prominent Redemptorist theologian, lecturer, and author of several exhortatory books, Father O. R. Vassall-Phillips. His attack was published in the *Southern Cross*, the local Catholic weekly newspaper, on 20 January 1932. Shaw evidently did not see the article in its entirety in this paper. It scarcely mattered. The *Cape Argus*, from which he obtained his information, quoted lengthy extracts in its report under the headline "Who Then Is This G.B.S.?"

This was the question Vassall-Phillips asked in launching himself against Shaw. He answered it by granting that Shaw had a "gift for writing good and nervous English, and above all plays that strike the imagination." These were scarcely unique qualities, and "when one has said this one has said practically all there is to be said about Mr Shaw which marks him off as in any way admirable." For the rest he was marked out from his fellow men by "almost incredible intellectual arrogance, his egolomania, which mounts to a pitch that probably has never been known in any other human being, and his passionate determination to get himself always into the limelight so that he may be talked about—as he would wish incessantly and to the depreciation of everybody else . . . the more extravagant his statements the better he seems pleased; to produce this effect, he will hesitate or stop at nothing, and seems to rejoice in making statements which he knows will be deeply offensive, whether on the grounds of religion or patriotism, to those who are bound by his persistence to listen to them. What good purpose will be served," Vassall-Phillips asked, "by writing in the 'Southern Cross' about Mr. Bernard Shaw?" He answered his question by asserting that there were unhappily a large number of persons who were likely, unless warned, to take him at his own valuation and to attach some importance to his words, which "must be taken—so he assumes—on his own ipse dixit—merely because he has said them. In his judgment on the capacity of his readers he is as arrogant and insolent as he is pretentious and crafty."

Vassall-Phillips then turned on Shaw for his statements about Christianity and sneered at him for his "piece of bluff" for saying that no educated man believed in Christianity and for being in his own estimation the supereducated man. More sneers followed, now about Shaw's "irresistible" gurgling chuckle. "Mr Shaw laughs at his own jokes," he says, his lip curled yet more, "I can well believe it. . . . Fly away and begone, Mr Shaw, with your irresistible chuckles. They are not in place. At least withdraw your imposture and general offensiveness from men in Cape Town who still believe in Christ and Christianity. . . . [Y]ou are not wanted."[15]

Shaw's reply appeared in the *Argus* the next evening, on 23 January:

You have given the currency of your large and unsectarian circulation for certain statements connected with my name by Father Vassall-Phillips in a Roman Catholic journal.

The first statement is that a large number of persons attach some importance to my words. I hope this is true; but I fear that Father Vassall-Phillips would be hard put to it to produce any practical evidence of it.

But, as he believes it to be true, he must also believe that, in claiming my authority for any sort of doctrine, he is giving importance to that doctrine.

He then claims my authority for the doctrine that no educated men believe in Christianity, because I do not believe in it myself.

Yet I gather from the rest of his article as quoted, that he does not wish to discredit Christianity, though he clearly does wish—very unchristianly—to discredit me.

In short, he uses the cross as a stick to beat me with, without stopping to consider what the effect of his assault will be on the large number of people who, he believes, will vote against Christianity if they are led to believe that I am opposed to it.

Now it is the way of priests to lose their heads when Christ is in question. They are unable to forget that they crucified him. And they seem equally unable to remember it.

If I venture, as I have done, to say a word on Christ's behalf, as against Barabbas, they rend their clothes and shriek "Blasphemy!" as of old.

But if I point out that Christ is still, as of old, despised and rejected of men, especially educated men, they warn people not to listen to me, as they have adopted Him and made Him respectable.

There is no pleasing them.

Anyone who is interested in my view of Christ and Christianity will find it set forth with all the lucidity I can command in the preface to my play, "Androcles and the Lion."

Of Father Vassall-Phillips's view I know nothing except what I gather from your quotations from his article.

I therefore have no right to criticise it at large. But all my cards are on the table; and I would rather like him, for the good of his soul, to study them before he calls me to judgment.[16]

Vassall-Phillips returned to the fray in the next issue of the *Southern Cross*. He assured his readers that he had no feeling about Shaw on private grounds, and that, had he come over from England on the same boat as Shaw, he had no doubt he would have found him an extremely agreeable person. This is hard to accept considering the charges of intellectual arrogance, "egolomania," insolence, and craftiness he had heaped on Shaw in the original attack. "But," he continued, "I have long watched his career and know him as a persistent enemy of what I believe to be Christian Faith and Morals, which I hold dearer than life." Some comments followed repudiating Shaw's remarks about priests, and then he admitted to not having read *Androcles and the Lion*. It was the interview in the

Cape Times on which he based his attack and to which he took exception, in particular the reference to Christ as an "idol."[17]

This is no retraction, but it does attempt to dampen the fire and brimstone of the original. Shaw is not likely to have seen this; neither does it matter, except that an editorial preamble to Father Vassall-Phillips's reply makes the point that Shaw's response in the *Argus* was an unusual course for him to adopt. This is so. Shaw would write to the newspapers, and write again—and again—in support of or opposition to one or other contentious issue of the day; but almost never did he write in defense of his personal image.[18] He never indulged in name-calling and simply shrugged it off when others engaged in this pastime at his expense. Yet here he was actually replying in the public press—reacting not to the personal attack so much as to the religious issue, and this in the middle of a sun-drenched, fruit-filled holiday. The temperate tone of the letter could suggest that he was taking the matter in his stride. This may not be so: Shaw's cards *were* on the table, but the incident could have triggered the thought that it was perhaps time to shuffle the deck and lay out the cards anew. Not many weeks hence the Black Girl would set out to find Shaw's God in the "virgin forest."

This letter was all Shaw wrote to the press during his and Charlotte's stay in Cape Town. He received a huge number of letters from South African admirers and occasional critics; he could not possibly respond to all that came in, and he had to resort to drafting hasty responses and turning them over to a part-time secretary.[19] His letters to friends at home and elsewhere seem to have been minimal: he and Charlotte were on holiday, after all. Even so, the *Collected Letters, 1926–1950* contains a few written from Cape Town and elsewhere in South Africa at this time, and one to Emery Walker, written a meager two weeks after his arrival, reveals the depths of Shaw's insights into and concern about the South African situation. "This place is full of sunshine, long days, and darkies to do all the work," he told Walker. "The Dutch Peter de Hooghe interiors are enchanting; but the social problems—poor whites competing for unskilled labor jobs with a black proletariat which can live on next to nothing, with no pensions, nor unemployment insurance, and race war between Dutch and English—are insoluble."[20]

The "darkies"—the disadvantaged "black proletariat"—to whom Shaw refers here were the so-called "Cape Coloreds," who comprised the vast majority of nonwhite peoples in the western Cape at the time. The product of three centuries of interracial breeding between white settlers and sailors and the nonwhite peoples of the Cape—those native to the country and those imported as slaves from the East—the "Coloreds" had the franchise but little or no economic or social status and were condemned, as Shaw saw all too clearly, by their history and circumstances to be at the bottom of the economic and social pile. As for the so-called "poor whites," they were largely the victims of drought and the Great Depression of the 1930s, which caused many in impoverished rural communities to move to the cities. That Shaw saw all this after so short a stay in the country—and in the most settled and culturally rich of South African cities—says a good deal about his perspicacity, and he had not encountered the blacks of the country yet in any significant numbers. Despite the gloomy conclusion to his letter to Emery Walker—"the social problems . . . are insoluble"—he would find a solution through his Black Girl before the year was out.

Shaw delivered his radio broadcast in the evening of Saturday, 6 February 1932.[21] A seasoned broadcaster by then, he probably took the occasion in his stride. The broadcasting authorities did not. His address to the University Lunch Club had been broadcast locally. This one was turned into a national event, which meant, in those relatively early days of "wireless," the linking of all the major broadcasting stations in the country by means of telephone. The *Cape Times* reported that "fifteen hundred miles of telephone wire carried his voice to broadcasting stations at Johannesburg, Durban, Pretoria and Bloemfontein, where his speech . . . was relayed." It was the first time this kind of link-up was carried out, and Shaw, evidently realizing this, made the most of his opportunity to speak to the nation at large.

He said he had been asked to say nice things about South Africa, but he begged to be excused. Saying nice things was not his business. Even so, he praised Cape Town as an extraordinarily pleasant place to live in. It was a suntrap. "So far so good. But . . . " And the reservations, gently inserted into his discourse, became increasingly tough and uncompromising. Suntraps had a powerful attraction for people with money, and Capetonians could, if they were shortsighted enough, prosper on the trade such people brought with them. "Now that is all well and good as long as their money lasts. But suppose it should suddenly dry up!" This had happened in Russia, he warned, where the once fabulously rich

people of that country—the grand dukes and the nobles and the pluto-
crats—were now driving taxis or cleaning boots in Paris. This could happen elsewhere; it could happen in South Africa. Not that he wanted to
frighten his listeners out of venturing their capital in building hotels and
delightful suburban dwellings. They would always come in useful.
Meanwhile, he said, "[A]bolish your slums, for which, let me tell you,
Cape Town deserves to be destroyed by fire from heaven."

Then it was on to agriculture and the need to change farming methods,
to obtain fertilizers from the air, and, in effect, for farmers and the country at large to prove they had more than tuppenny-ha'penny minds by
collectivizing farming land and getting the state to stump for developments in agriculture. South Africans "are much less fat-headed than
people in England," he said. "The men are bigger and the women better
and younger looking. I should say they all have thousand pound minds.
But the jobs in front of them will run into hundreds of millions in mental
as well as metal capacity; and that will cost them a little more in thinking
exercise and a little less surf-bathing."

This brought him to another warning: "Suppose the gold gives out
and diamonds come down to six a penny?" Where then would South
Africa be? A holiday-maker's paradise and industrially barren? Such
earthly paradises had their place in the scheme of things; only take care:

If I were to spend a couple of years in Cape Town my character
would be fatally undermined. I should never do another day's honest work. . . . And that brings me to a very serious part of the business. One of the first things I noticed when I landed was that I immediately became dependent on the services of men and women
who are not of my own color. I felt that I was in a Slave State, and
that, too, the very worst sort of Slave State. I mean the sort in which
the slaves are not owned by masters who are responsible for their
welfare, nor protected by stringent laws from ill-treatment, but one
in which they are nominally free, like white people, and can be
thrown into the streets to starve, without pensions or public relief,
when nobody happens to need their services or when they are old
and are displaced by the young. This state of things makes wise
people uneasy. Foolish people think that the danger is that the slaves
will rebel and refuse to do any more work. But that is not the real
danger at all; and even if it were it would not matter, because white

men can still easily suppress rebellions even if they have to employ black men to help them. No, the real snag in the business is that if you let other people do everything for you, you will soon become incapable of doing anything for yourself.

You become an idler and a parasite, a weakling and an imbecile; and though you may also become a very pretty lady or gentleman you will be helpless in the hands of your slaves, who will have all the strength and knowledge and character that come from working and from nothing else. He can reduce you to that condition, so that you cannot do without him. Even the things that you still can do for yourself he can make you ashamed to do. He actually dictates your ideas of right and wrong, respectable and disreputable, until you are his mental as well as his bodily slave, while all the time you flatter yourself that you are his lord and master. I fancy that I have seen one or two very nice-looking and nicely-dressed young people in Cape Town who are in some danger of drifting into this most un-happy condition. If their parents brought them up to it, and to be proud of it, their parents deserve to be shot.

There is only one way of escaping this fate where slavery exists, whether the slavery be black or poor white. Take my own case. The slave who fetches and carries for me, who cooks and sweeps and dusts for me, who does rough, muscular or mechanical work for me, sets me free to do work of a higher kind just as surely as to idle and loaf. If I do the higher work the slave will look up to me and never grudge me his service if I acknowledge its value to me and treat him decently. In fact his industry will no longer be slavery, for we shall both be doing our bit, I for him and he for me. But if I make the downward choice and idle and loaf, woe betide me; for there is no future now in the world for idlers and loafers. If white civilization breaks down through idleness and loafing based on slavery—and remember that modern historical research has discovered that half a dozen civilizations like ours have broken down through just that canker in them—then, as likely as not, the next great civilization will be a negro civilization. Anyhow, black or white, it will be built up by workers, not by parasite ladies and gentlemen.

This said, Shaw turned to more pleasing matters, thanking the many people who had written to him and apologizing for not having been able to respond to every letter. He did not forget to mention several well-wishers who had asked him "very earnestly" where he would spend eternity, reminding these folk that the question was not in his hands, and that, anyway, he was in eternity already. In conclusion: "I broadcast my thanks to you from a heart full of gratitude and a stomach full of peaches. Good night and good luck."

The kernel of his address is in the admonitory section, and it is interesting to trace some of his thoughts here to their origins in Shaw's writings. His socialist philosophy underlies everything he said about the Capetonian "suntrap," as it underscored everything he said or did throughout his adult life. The dangers inherent in such a "trap"—making a living out of the sale of luxuries, the creation of idlers, loafers, and parasites—are adumbrated in *The Apple Cart*, where Britain's economy is described as being sustained by the manufacture and export of luxury goods. *Back to Methuselah* touches on two issues mentioned here, the possibility of a black civilization superseding the present white one and—a characteristic paradox—the creation of a slave state in which the masters are the slaves and the slaves are the masters. And the 1901 essay "Civilization and the Soldier" foresees the disintegration of white civilization during the twentieth century.[22] All this went into *The Black Girl* in extended form; all this plus Mabel Shaw, plus Father Vassall-Phillips, plus a lifetime—some seventy-five years—of experience and thought. Shaw's mind was nothing if not a grand accumulator and sifter of impressions. He was ready, although he did not know it yet, to write *The Black Girl*. All he still lacked was a suitable setting and protagonist.

The day after the broadcast, on Sunday, 7 February 1932, Shaw, Charlotte, and their companion-guide, Commander C. P. Newton of the Cape Town Publicity Bureau, left Cape Town by car, bound for Port Elizabeth, some five hundred miles to the east. They would then embark for Durban and continue along the east coast of Africa through Suez and the Mediterranean back to England. Or that was their intention, that their plan.

3

Accident

Off they went, over mountain passes and across rolling coastal plains, the sea a frequent glittering expanse on their right. They took the "Garden Route," so called because of its breathtaking scenery and, for those who had eyes to see, the wildflowers unique to the Cape. It is likely that Shaw, never one for scenic "oohs" and "aahs," did not have eyes for this; his interest was in the driving. Having taken and passed his driving test in Cape Town and been issued a license—an indulgent act, one is inclined to think, prompted by his celebrity—he was determined to take his turn behind the wheel.

Charlotte's skimpy entries in her engagement book cum diary for the year are all one has to go on for the next few days:[1]

> Sunday 7th Feb. 1932: Up early. Packing. Leave Cape Town. Get to Caledon about 1:30. Lunched there. On to Swellendam before dinner where we slept.
> Monday 8th Feb. 1932: Left 9:15 up into the Karroo—up long gorge and over pass to [indecipherable]. Great heat. Over another wonderful pass to Oudschoorn where we slept in hotel.
> Tuesday 9th Feb. 1932: Left about 10. GBS drove over very beautiful pass & down to the sea by George to Wilderness—others bathed, Mr Grant (head of hotel) with them.
> Wednesday 10th Feb. 1932: Left Wilderness about 9. Accident. Came to Royal Hotel, Knysna (Fraser).

After this, from Thursday, 11 February 1932, to Wednesday, 16 March 1932, the only entry is "Ill at Knysna."

It is not easy to trace the trip with precision. Charlotte is on target with her place names, if not always with her spelling, but she is vague about other matters: the route taken, for instance, and the names of the hotels in Oudtshoorn and Wilderness. Roads and routes have been considerably altered since 1932, and the "long gorge" and pass of 8 February may no longer be quite what the touring party negotiated. The main point is that they took a wide detour to Oudtshoorn, famous in its day for its ostrich farming and production of feathers for the haut monde of Europe.[2] They probably traveled through the Robinson Pass to get there and when returning (with Shaw driving) took the Outeniqua Pass to Wilderness. Shaw would not have known it yet, but in arriving at Wilderness—a lush coastal region backed by dense forest and looking out on foaming seas—he was on the outskirts of the Black Girl's territory. And it was the next day, approaching Knysna with Shaw driving, that the accident occurred.

He drove the car off the road, and—as is averred in authoritative accounts of the incident—he actually went faster, mistaking the accelerator for the brake. His own accounts almost admit this but are somewhat self-exculpatory on the whole. As he told the *Cape Times* in a telegram correcting their correspondent's account of the mishap:

> I most indignantly deny that I drove into a ditch.
> I have never done such a thing. I cleared
> a ditch;
> a hedge;
> a fence;
> a formidable bunker;
> and several minor cross-country obstacles when the ingenious construction of an apparently safe and straight stretch of South African road deflected me into the veld.
> I challenge your Mossel Bay correspondent to emulate that feat.[3]

One may take this for what it is worth—a bit of swank, a touch of face-saving blarney, perhaps also an attempt to deflect public attention away from him and Charlotte captive in Knysna; but the accident was no minor matter. Shaw and Newton next to him in the passenger seat were unhurt, but Charlotte in the back was flung forward, pieces of luggage tumbling over her, leaving her badly bruised and shaken. They were rushed to Knysna, where, fortuitously, they had decided to spend some days; although it was not thought necessary to place Charlotte in a hospital, she was confined to her bed in the Royal Hotel. Shaw, fearing a deluge of reporters and other unwanted enquirers, tried to minimize both her injuries and the accident itself, at least as far as public announcements went. He told Blanche Patch, his secretary back home, something of the truth: "The injuries are only bruises and sprains and a troublesome hole in the shin plus two black eyes." One notes the "only." Blanche Patch was not taken in. "Quite enough," she remarked, "for a venerable lady of seventy-six."[4] Shaw was less reticent in his letter to Lady Rhondda, written in Knysna five days after the accident. "All our plans for the East Coast have been upset by a sensational exploit of mine which has miraculously escaped the papers, and which you must hide in your bosom to save us from a deluge of enquiries. . . . I negotiated several mountain ranges and gorges in a masterly manner; but on what I thought a perfectly safe bit of straight road I indulged in a turn of speed and presently got violently deflected into an overcorrected spin. . . . I got off with a crack on the chin from the steering wheel and a clip on the knee. But Charlotte! I can't describe it. Broken head, two black eyes, sprained left arm, bruised back, and a hole in her shin not so deep as a well nor so wide as a church door— but let me not think on't."[5]

In fact, the newspapers of the world, the London *Times* and the *New York Times* among them, did report the accident, though not in the Shakespearean accents Shaw adopted. Anxious friends telephoned, but the feared deluge of newspaper enquiries did not materialize, and Shaw's desire for privacy seems to have been respected on the whole. Knysna was very remote, with telephone communication difficult, and well beyond the purview of metropolitan newshounds.

The arrival of the Shaws and the circumstances surrounding it caused quite a ripple in Knysna itself. The editor of the local four-page weekly, the *Knysna Advertiser,* could barely contain his excitement and featured Shaw in a long article in which he described a trip Shaw took into the forest and made a good deal of not telling his readers what had caused this famous man to stop over in their town. He promised a second article for the following week, but nothing appeared, and it is likely he was prevailed on to refrain. Not entirely deterred, he kept the local community aware of the continuing presence of the great man by inserting admiring reports and comments in his paper for the duration of Shaw and Charlotte's stay in Knysna. The other country newspaper, the *George and Knysna Herald,* produced in George sixty miles away, also carried brief weekly reports on the Shaws—Charlotte, for example, was reported to be up and about by early March—and one or two articles, but like its counterpart in Knysna left them alone. It seems that both Shaw and Charlotte took to the medical practitioner, Dr Jack Allen, who attended Charlotte; there was some socializing—he and his wife, Irene, had the Shaws to dinner when Charlotte was well enough to go out, and Shaw read one of his plays to them.[6] Shaw accompanied him on some of his rounds in the district, so getting to know the region and its rural communities: the Afrikaner farmers, the "Colored" and black laborers, and the woodcutters of the Knysna forest (the "degenerates" Shaw mentioned in his final interview).

Legend provides the most entertaining tidbits: a manifestly unclad Shaw was regularly observed striding back and forth in front of his open hotel window, to the mingled awe and delight of the local populace, while his daily dip in the Knysna lagoon—to which he was driven by the hotel manager, Fraser—was similarly revealing. These legends linger on, seventy years after the event.

It was then, once they were settled in their hotel and Charlotte was reasonably comfortable, that Shaw began to think of resuming work by writing . . . a play, as he told Newton, if he could think of a suitable topic. Within three days he had started, not on a play but on what became *The Adventures of the Black Girl in Her Search for God.* Dan H. Laurence relates that for a third of a century Shaw had contemplated writing "a big book of devotion for modern people," as he described it to his amateur photographer friend Frederick Evans in a letter of 1895, "bringing all the truths latent in the old religious dogmas into contact with real life—a gospel of Shawianity, in fact." (He also had it in mind, he told Evans in the same letter, to write a book of erotica, but nothing seems to have come of this ambition.) Laurence continues: "What finally emerged . . . was a compact cosmic fable that effectively blended Lewis Carroll and Voltaire with the Bible."[7] Lewis Carroll? *Alice's Adventures in Wonderland* and *Through the Looking Glass* can well be seen to anticipate the fantastic elements of *The Black Girl,* particularly in their depiction of caricatures. As for the "gospel of Shawianity," it gives one pause to realize that a conscious intention of some thirty-seven years before should come to fruition (in considerably modified form) in 1932 and in Knysna.

One should consider first the impact the local scene made on Shaw, which was considerable. His protagonist is female and black. Mabel Shaw's little charges in distant Mbereshi Mission were females, and perhaps this had something to do with Shaw's choice of gender. It is more likely that his decision was based on what he observed of the young black women of the district. These observations, plus his strong feminism and his awareness of the role played by the female in the teleology of life, would have dictated his choice. His other option—a male—is not plausible or persuasive. For one thing, Voltaire's antihero had already played that part, and a Shavian Candide would have seemed derivative and contrived. For another, one cannot seriously imagine such a youth venturing into the forest on a religious quest; a sexual assignation would have been more in his line. So from all points of view—biological, psychological, and artistic—his protagonist had to be female. As for her being native to the country, Shaw first encountered black Africans as distinct from the "Cape Coloreds" in significant numbers when in Knysna, and his first, repeatedly expressed, impression of them was that they had far better manners than the whites and were more dignified and graceful. His admiration suggests Rousseau's "noble savage"—another eighteenth-century image—in his depiction of the Black Girl, except that she is no "savage." It is the whites who are the "savages." She is a young black, probably Xhosa, woman; in Shaw's words, she is "a fine creature, whose satin skin and shining muscles made the white missionary folk seem like ashen ghosts by contrast."[8] The contrast and a good deal more emerge strongly in her various encounters, nowhere more strongly than in her confrontation with members of the Caravan of the Curious and the Arab.[9] Shaw idealizes her, a necessary measure in view of the roles he will assign her to perform during her quest. He also departs from custom in arming her with a knobkerry, which no black woman would carry. In his reactive pamphlet titled *Adventures of the White Girl in Her Search for God*, one of Shaw's critics, C. H. Maxwell, remarked disdainfully on this "lapse," which, he said, justified his protagonist's use of a golfing iron in her quest. However, Shaw had his precedent in Athena, and besides, his Black Girl is an exceptional individual.

Shaw was no Keats, still less a Shakespeare, when it came to naming trees and plants, so the forest the Black Girl enters is simply that, with little or nothing in the text to suggest or identify its arboreal and floral splendors. Perhaps this is as it should be, a green and verdant place with shadows numberless, the haunt of mystery and myth, quite unspecific and "virgin"—a reversion to the Garden of Eden before the Fall. This setting is certainly inspired by the dense coastal forest—the Tsitsikamma—that surrounds Knysna.

It is inhabited by a few creatures of the forest: a mamba, one of the most poisonous of snakes; and a spitting snake, the ringhals, both of which cooperatively and in turn—and rather in the false manner of the serpent in Genesis—lead the Black Girl to two different versions of "God." The snakes are themselves stand-ins, together with other personalities, for the Tree of Knowledge, which in Shaw becomes the Tree of Error. Shaw erred in his original depiction of the ringhals, where it was credited with possessing a rattle, like its American cousin. Someone put him right, and what the original text has as "she disturbed a rattlesnake or ringhals, which was gliding away when she said 'Well, Clicky-clicky: you are not so ill-natured as the mamba'" became in revision, "she disturbed a sort of cobra called a ringhals, which spat at her." There are other minor changes on this page ("Clicky-clicky" becoming "Spitty-spitty," for example), but, in short, Shaw's revisions did not disturb the layout of the page, an important consideration.[10] There is also a lion the Black Girl addresses familiarly as "Dicky." (Is he meant to represent King Richard Lion-Heart? Not quite, although he is called "Richard" in the text. Shaw named him after a friendly lion at the London zoo, as he told his illustrator, John Farleigh). Shaw described Dicky in his text as a maneless lion and insisted that Farleigh copy Landseer's lions in Trafalgar Square, that is to say he wanted a lion with a handsome, orderly (and appropriately regal) arrangement of hair, not a "touzled mop,"[11] which is the usual tonsorial style of the male lion. It is hard to see how else a sculptor (Landseer) or a wood engraver (Farleigh) would recreate a lion's mane in their respective mediums other than by avoiding that "mop" and making it orderly and regal. More to the immediate point, if there were lions in the Tsitsikamma Forest in 1932, they were few and far between, fugitive beasts doomed to succumb soon to the hunter's gun and the trapper's snare. Dr Jack Allen and others who took him on trips into the district may well have embroidered their account of the wild life in the forest for their credulous companion; they would certainly have told Shaw about the elephants, of which there were a fair number at the time, and one regrets not witnessing a meeting between this most sagacious of animals and the Black Girl, even though it is mentioned in passing as being prone to trample on people. Any such meeting would have lacked biblical sanction however, whereas the lion crops up frequently—not in Genesis but later as a heraldic beast denoting fierceness; as Samson's luckless adversary; as Daniel's remarkably laid-back companions during his night with them; and as a touchstone of vengeful fierceness in Jeremiah's jeremiads, in which a lion is forever lurking in the forest or the thicket, ready to pounce on and devour the sinful sons and daughters of Judah. But here, in *The Black Girl*, Dicky is out-lioned by the Lion of Judah, so to speak, the prophet Micah, and he flees into the forest to escape the horrific roaring this volcanic fellow with a "number six nose" sets up.[12] Apart from this and from imparting a touch of actuality to the setting, Dicky does not seem to serve any special function in the plot, except perhaps to suggest that the beasts of the forest will turn tail and flee when a prophet of the Lord of Hosts rages and roars.

What about the crocodile? There he is in Farleigh's illustration, with a shortsighted gentleman sitting on him. The crocodile has a toothy smile and is looking up at the "myop" in a considering way, as though he has solved the problem of what to have for dinner. But, of course, he is not really there; he is a fiction created by the Black Girl to catch the "myop" out in his bogus science of the conditioned reflex.

So much for the natural history worked into the story. It is not much, but it manages to suggest Africa in certain wild and virginal aspects. There are also a few verbal South Africanisms, mainly of Dutch-Afrikaans origin. "Ringhals" (literally, "ring neck"), which identifies the snake by the yellow circlet, or ring, below its hood, is one; "knobkerry," or "knobkerrie" (Shaw is inconsistent in his spelling)—the cudgel with which the Black Girl arms herself before setting out on her quest—is another; "tickey," meaning a threepenny bit, is a third. Shaw seems to have been taken with this last word. His conjuror uses it: "But [people] refuse to believe me unless I do conjuring tricks for them; and when I do them they only throw me coppers and sometimes tickeys." "What is a tickey?" his companion, an Arab, asks. "A threepenny bit," says the conjuror. "It is coined because proud people are ashamed to be seen giving me coppers, and they think sixpence too much."[13] There are also "baas" and "piccaninny" and the "girl" of the title, but more will be said about these words in chapter 7, where I consider the question of verbal political correctness.

Shaw wrote most, if not all, of *The Black Girl* in about eighteen days. As in Cape Town, he made use of a local stenographer, Dorothy Smith, who remembered their association with keen pleasure. "He never made me feel he was the great G.B.S., but always thanked me as if I were doing him a favour. I must confess I liked him exceedingly."[14]

What happens in *The Black Girl*? Aspects of the plot have been touched on; no coherent summary has been provided, however. The best is Shaw's own as given to his friend Dame Laurentia McLachlan, the abbess of Stanbrook.[15]

"The story," he tells her, "is about a negro girl converted by a missionary, who takes her conversion very seriously and demands where she is to find God. 'Seek and ye shall find Him' is the only direction she gets; so off she goes through the forest on her search, with her knobkerrie in her hand. Her search is only too successful." Here Shaw lists the Black Girl's encounters, not in quite the sequence given in the final text, which scarcely matters. There is first the god of Abraham, then the god of Job— "and I regret to say she disposes of both with her knobkerrie"—then Ecclesiastes the Preacher, and Micah, and Pavlov, "who assures her that there is no god and that life is only a series of reflexes," and Saint Peter carrying a cathedral made of paper on his shoulders, and several others with paper churches who begin to throw stones at one another, forcing the Black Girl to run away. Then she meets Saint John clamoring for the promised Second Coming, then a Roman soldier guarding the symbol of Roman justice, the cross. She settles the soldier's high-and-mightiness with her knobkerry, then comes to the well of the woman of Samaria and finds, as Shaw tells Dame Laurentia, "your friend there, whom people call The Conjuror, as they wont listen to his preaching but like his miracles." This conjuror gives the Black Girl his commandment, love one another, which the Black Girl finds unsatisfactory because there are people whom she hates and ought to hate. Her next encounter is with an expedition of European scientists, the Caravan of the Curious, who squabble among themselves about the nature of the universe. The expedition includes "some rather unpleasant women," one of whom the Black Girl lays out with her knobkerry. Then it is back to the conjuror, now posing for an image maker by reclining comfortably on a cross. An Arab (Mohammed) is present, and he, the conjuror on the cross, and the image maker discuss the question of salvation while the Black Girl stands by contributing an occasional observation. The Arab invites the Black Girl to join his harem, but this involves him in a vigorous feminist argument in which he comes off second best. "The girl then goes off, declaring that when men begin talking about women they are unbearable. She presently comes to a villa with a garden, which a frightfully intelligent looking but wizened old gentleman (Voltaire) is cultivating in a rather amateurish way. On hearing of her quest, he remonstrates with her for her audacity and confesses that if someone told him that God was going to pay him a visit he should hide in the nearest mouse hole. Then he tells her the story of Jupiter and Semele. 'Besides,' he says, 'you need not trouble to hunt for God: he is always at your elbow.' This impresses her so much that she goes into the garden, and helps the old gentleman to cultivate it until he dies and bequeaths it to her."

This was apparently as far as Shaw had got with his story by early April 1932, after his and Charlotte's return to England. He had been mulling over the conclusion, and, as he confided to Dame Laurentia: "I am not sure that I shall not add another adventure with a person whom I shall call the Irishman."

The Irishman was added to the story, and in due course he marries the Black Girl, begetting a small tribe of charmingly coffee-colored children with her while continuing Voltaire's exemplary practice of cultivating the garden, though now in a modern more socialistic way.

Shaw's outline of the plot brings out the simplicity of the tale and its allegorical underpinning. He had said in his response to Vassall-Phillips's attack on him that his religious cards were on the table and had been there for many years. Here he is laying them out once again. If Dame Laurentia was his immediate audience in this summary, others were a presence: Vasssall-Phillips for one, Mabel Shaw for another; also all those well-intentioned folk who were forever writing to ask where he thought he would spend eternity. And, as he would say more than once in South Africa, the "Dutch"—that is to say the Afrikaners—had most urgent need to update their religious beliefs. The Bible should be banned and taken away from them, he said. They depended too much on it. He had written *The Black Girl* purely for the advantage of the "Boer."[16] Poppycock, of course, but like all Shaw's "poppycock," it contained a kernel of truth, in that, as he saw the "Boers," their rigid fundamentalism was holding them back in the eighteenth century. "Fundamentalist" *The Black Girl* assuredly was not.

A minor mystery surrounds Shaw's and Charlotte's movements in March, once Charlotte was well enough to be up and about. Writing to Blanche Patch on 17 February, a week after the accident, Shaw tells her that he has "made up my mind to stay here [at the Royal Hotel in Knysna] until the wound in [Mrs Shaw's] shin heals and then remain at a very pleasant place in the neighborhood called Wilderness until she is quite herself again."[17] The pleasant place called Wilderness could be the hotel, unnamed in Charlotte's diary, at which they had stayed on their way to Knysna. It could also refer to a private home, or homes, in that area. The Shaws did visit hospitable friends, though whether for a few hours only or for longer periods is impossible to ascertain. The evening with Dr Jack Allen and his wife in Knysna has been mentioned; the *George and Knysna Herald* mentions a visit by Shaw and Charlotte to a certain Major Pullar of Fancourt, near George, on the eve of their departure from George; and there is even an unsubstantiated report in a local guidebook that they were the guests of the prime minister, General Hertzog, at a private holiday residence at Wilderness. Whatever their comings and goings, Shaw and Charlotte's hosts and Shaw himself maintained a tight-lipped silence. Privacy was to be maintained—except in one instance, where a teenage son—his identity hidden in a cryptic "Hu OHS George"—reported on the afternoon that Shaw visited his parents at their seaside cottage at Wilderness. This was probably on 10 February, Shaw having driven from Oudtshoorn that morning. This report appeared in the *George and Knysna Herald* of 24 February. It does not say much, although it conveys something of the momentousness of the occasion for the youngster and rather charmingly expresses his personal disappointment in not having been able to entertain the family's distinguished guest with a piano recital, on account of an injured finger. Another report-cum-comment appeared as the first leader in the same paper a week after the Shaw's departure. It details Shaw's very short stay in George on 17 March, the day before he and Charlotte flew back to Cape Town, and remarks on the effect of this visit on the good townsfolk of George. It is a chatty piece in which the editor implausibly relates how he encountered Shaw in the street and soon had him seated in the newspaper's "inner sanctum" talking about this and that.[18]

It was comical to reflect that a couple of weeks earlier two visiting clergymen in the very same chairs had been warmly debating whether Shaw could possibly be a gentleman. We had no wish to "interview" him in the ordinary sense, because we . . . knew there were very few houses where his opinions would be welcome. Most people hate the agony of thinking, and there is nothing they dislike more than being disturbed in their old ideas and the sense of personal comfort. And Mr Shaw can be very provoking. Our visitor was naturally interested, . . . [having] spent several weeks of his short stay in South Africa in these quiet backwaters where religious routine and human stagnation appear to him to go hand in hand. . . .

. . . Mr Shaw's outlook is critical and destructive of the old images—the mental furniture of past generations—and that is why his views are so heartily disliked in some quarters. "I do hope you disapprove of Mr Shaw," said one lady when we dropped in.

One wonders what this lady would have said had she known about the typescript in Shaw's luggage.

After a night at the Hotel Victoria in George, the Shaws were taken to the airfield; the *George and Knysna Herald* went on to relate: "And on Friday morning, about ten o'clock, the shining all-metal Junkers' flying machine from Windhoek alighted on the George aerodrome. Mr Shaw had chartered the big bus to take his wife and himself to Cape Town, to catch the 'Warwick Castle' that afternoon for England. Mrs Shaw, now happily recovered from the motor mishap, carried a bunch of roses, and there was a fine basket of fruit, and a little crowd to say goodbye."

Off they went, back to Cape Town, then from the airport to the *Warwick Castle* in Cape Town harbor. The visit was not quite over yet. An *Argus* and possibly other reporters followed Shaw on board and secured (or were handed) a final "interview."

South Africa was dull though beautiful, Shaw said. "If I told you the whole truth about it you would never publish it." He had seen more of the people of South Africa since being out in the country, particularly the "Dutch"—the Afrikaners—who were, he thought, a fine upstanding race, particularly well built and interesting "because they have been so long isolated from the world." All they needed was education; make them, he said, take an interest in things and be intelligent. "And, above all, ban the Bible. . . . They depend too much on it." He went on:

I do not think your natives are psychologically more interesting than the white races. But they are more intelligent—they are the only people who can do your work—and they have far better manners.

You ask me whether South Africa will ever "go native." I think the question should be: "Will the native ever go South African?" He seems to get little opportunity of doing so.

You ask me whether South Africa needs a five-year plan. . . . This country does not need a five-year plan. You have too much self-denial already. There are thousands of people in the country starving—thousands of natives with scarcely enough food to keep them alive. . . .

What you want to do is shoot your poor whites—every one of them. You should also shoot many of your rich whites.

At Knysna . . . I came on large numbers of absolutely degenerate people—people with no intelligence, absolutely hopeless as stock for South Africa. You ought to shoot them all.

He touched on his new work. "It is not a book at all—it is merely a large pamphlet which an enterprising publisher would make into a book. It deals with a native girl's search for God."[19]

It was not an affable farewell. Disgruntled and rather trigger-happy though he may have been, Shaw could count a few pluses: Charlotte had recovered, he was fit and well—and he had written that "large pamphlet."

Publication

On the face of it, Shaw's reference to a "suitable publisher" for *The Black Girl* was just talk. He was his own publisher, and the firm that brought out his books and marketed them in Britain, Constable of London, was—if not absolutely in thrall to him—fully aware of his worth and more than willing to fall in with his requirements. This had not always been easy for them, for Shaw was nothing if not demanding, but the association had worked to the considerable benefit of the parties involved for nearly thirty years. In spite of this, Shaw had initial doubts about publication of his "pamphlet" under the Constable imprint and hesitated before taking the plunge.

He wrote to Otto Kyllman, one of the directors of Constable, within a week of his and Charlotte's return to England, telling him that he had written a story, "or rather a Voltairean pamphlet, very blasphemous, describing a negro girl's search for God." He thought he would add it unobtrusively to the *Standard Edition* of the short stories, "after turning an honest penny by serializing it if I can get anyone to venture on it."[1] This was on 9 April; on 14 April, he sent a typescript of the tale to his printer in Edinburgh, R. and R. Clark, telling the firm that he did not know what he would do with his Black Girl story, but that Clark might as well set it up as it would come out in the *Standard Edition* short-story volume sooner or later, and anyway it would be a great convenience to him to have a half dozen proofs forthwith. Clark responded at once, and Shaw received his proof copies, date-stamped 20 April, well before the end of the month. He sent a copy to his friend the "Red" dean of St Paul's, W. R. Inge, with an inscription in which Shaw said that, whether inspired to write the book "from above or below," he did not know what to do with "the thing." He sent another copy to Dame Laurentia McLachlan, who had "demanded" to see the work (Shaw having told her about it before-hand), inscribing the flyleaf as follows:

An Inspiration
which came in response to the prayers of the nuns
of Stanbrook Abbey
and
in particular
to the prayers of his dear Sister Laurentia
for
Bernard Shaw

Laurence continues:

> About a fortnight after this, Shaw sent to Dame Laurentia a little play, which she interpreted to mean that he was scrapping the work (as in fact he may momentarily have considered doing in light of his indecision as to its publication). "You have made me happy again by your nice little play," she wrote to him on 3rd May, "and I thank you from my heart for listening to me. I have read most of the book and I agree with many of your ideas, but if you had published it, I could never have forgiven you. However you are going to be good and I feel light & springy again & proud of my dear Brother Bernard. You shall have more prayers by way of reward! .... I simply cannot find words to thank you for your answer to my letter, but you *know* how grateful I am."

The "little play" Laurence refers to—the "letter" of 2 May to Dame Laurentia—is ambiguous as to Shaw's intentions, to say the least.[2] But, in spite of the moral pressure Dame Laurentia was exerting on him, he was keeping his options open.

The director of R. and R. Clark, William Maxwell, read *The Black Girl* while it was being set up and liked it, telling Shaw it could make an attractive and saleable book with the addition of some striking illustrations. He recommended a young wood engraver, John Farleigh, for the task.[3] Shaw wrote to Farleigh immediately. "The idea is that you and I and Maxwell should co-operate in turning out a goodlooking little volume consisting of the story contained in the enclosed proof sheets (please hold them as very private and confidential) and, say, a dozen pictures." Shaw included a check for five guineas and twelve "Suggested Subjects," among these, "4) The lion 'maneless' like Landseer's lions in Trafalgar Square. There used to be a delightful one named Dick in the zoo who would let you handle him as in the story. . . . 6) Sundry faces from the Caravan of the Curious, like the Vanity Fair jury in the Pilgrim's Progress—if you have a weakness for the ugly-grotesque and 10) Voltaire (after Houdon) digging with the girl looking at him over the garden gate."[4] Maxwell had triggered Shaw's visual imagination to such effect that in the end these three examples and the other nine proffered suggestions all featured in the book. Thus was begun the soon-to-be famous partnership between a world-renowned author and a relatively unknown illustrator of books.

Maxwell did something else for Shaw without realizing it: he enabled Shaw to override his scruples regarding Dame Laurentia McLachlan's stern admonition: "but if you had published it, I could never have forgiven you." One cannot imagine Shaw dismissing this lightly; he held Dame Laurentia in high regard, but something more than her displeasure and disappointment was urging him on. Was it a lust for yet more notoriety? This is not at all likely. Was it the thought of a possible sales windfall? If a consideration—and one must remember that Shaw earned his living as a playwright-writer—it could scarcely have been more than a passing one. It was deeply held conviction, profound faith, or, if one likes, the spirit of Voltaire asserting itself in Shaw.

The account that follows is derived largely from John Farleigh's memoir, *Graven Image*.[5] In his early thirties in 1932 and by no means an established artist, indeed struggling to make an impression—any kind of impression—on publishers, Farleigh would have viewed this letter from Shaw and the invitation that went with it as an unexpected windfall. As he modestly put it, "I am asked: 'Did you know Bernard Shaw? Then how did you get his book to illustrate?' Oddly enough, I wonder that myself."[6] His first reaction on receiving the letter was wonderment that Shaw should apparently owe him five guineas; his second that no, this was not a hoax but the real thing; his third that "here was a great chance for illustration"; and his fourth, once he had skimmed through the text, that Shaw had demonstrated unerring skill in stimulating the excitement of any illustrator and providing in his twelve suggestions what Farleigh saw as an "excellent and complete theme."

"Here," he said to himself, "was a small masterpiece as good as Voltaire's *Candide* and as seductive to the palette of an illustrator as any book could be." Shaw had invited him to submit a trial drawing. Farleigh chose suggestion 8, which was "Christ posing on the cross for sixpence an hour with the image maker (say yourself) at work, and Mahomet, very handsome, looking on."[7] "With the best will in the world," he said, "no artist can do himself justice in a trial drawing or rough." But Farleigh tried his best and—plainly fired by the opportunity presenting itself to him—produced an excellent effort, even though it took him a full two weeks to complete. He sent it to Shaw and anxiously awaited the verdict. The reply came: "Good: I think you can make a real job of it." After this, Shaw got down to business. He wanted the right to reproduce all over the globe during the whole term of copyright as "illustrations to the book." He would pay Farleigh a lump sum for this right and invited him to quote a figure. "This is the most irksome part of the affair; but it's got to be done. So sit down and get it over." There was a postscript to the effect that Farleigh did not need to assign copyright to Shaw, and that he could regard the drawings as his provided they were presented separately from the story.

Farleigh met William Maxwell; then it was lunch with the Shaws at Whitehall Court "to discuss page and print." Conversation over lunch was about everything but "The Book." Then, at 2:45, they got down to business, and Farleigh—having already made up his mind about the typeface, the kind of paper to be used, and the removal of headlines from the pages—found Shaw conceding these points with surprising meekness and telling him to "Do it yourself." Farleigh recalled that, leaving Whitehall Court that afternoon and passing one of Landseer's lions in Trafalgar Square ("who looked even more friendly"), he found himself dwelling on a certain image in a curiously persistent way: "a small carved 'totem' of Shaw" in the Whitehall Court apartment. Perhaps, he thought, he would put this totem into the book somewhere. And he did, or rather one like it, as the front cover design of *The Black Girl* as first published in 1932 (since reproduced opposite the title page), where the Shaw totem may be discerned lurking among the ferns of the forest in the company of other totems, the crucified Christ among them.

It was not long before Shaw sent Farleigh a drawing—"the first of a series Shaw was to make for this job." Farleigh praised Shaw's efforts, not because they were technically skillful—they were not—but "because the visual power behind them was extraordinary: they contained everything that was necessary to make his point clear." At a later stage of the book, talking to Shaw on the phone, he told him his drawing had improved so much that he would not be needing him, Farleigh, before long. Shaw replied, "I did not set out to be Shakespeare, but Michelangelo!"

The days, weeks, the months went by, and on 6 July 1932, Shaw criticized Farleigh's initial depiction of the Black Girl: "Just consider whether she is not—for so critical a god-seeker—a little too brutish." She was indeed "too brutish," a far cry from the shapely, clear-eyed, high-browed god-seeker—her brow a palpable copy of Shaw's own high forehead—Farleigh would go on to create, to Shaw's evident satisfaction. A week later, on 13 July, he is discussing the endpapers and asking Farleigh not to bother about what he says: "it is your job and being an artist myself in my own line, I know better than to find a good man and then to interfere with him." In the same letter, he comments on the Roman soldier on guard at the cross, the picture to contain "a bucketful of nails, scourges, thorn crowns, etc. . . . It would serve him right if a knobkerry, grasped in a black hand, appeared over his unconscious head like the sword of Damocles." He added: "However, I repeat, let yourself rip, and do not let me hamper or distract you." This openhanded invitation was hedged in a few days later, on 18 July, when he criticized Farleigh's soldier for being secondhand Italian Renaissance. Farleigh did a new drawing of the Roman soldier, and Shaw pronounced it "perfect."

Time was passing. July became August, and Shaw in Malvern "cobbling up [his] play" (*Too True to Be Good*) was not able to attend to Farleigh's new batch of drawings immediately. His response, when it came and in spite of the distraction of the play, was as focused as ever. "The lion and the Job are perfect. . . . Ecclesiastes looks dead, like a figure in a frieze, because he is not looking at the girl. He also looks flat, like a profile cut in cardboard. All you have to do is turn his head away from the spectator and towards the girl and all this will come right."

This was followed by constructive criticism of the picture of the cathedrals, then on to consider Farleigh's Christ. He thought Farleigh had reversed the roles of the Christ and the Black Girl. "The smiling Christ is a great chance for you. Most artists are so utterly floored by the problem of what Christ's face ought to express that they just make it express nothing at all and cover up the failure with a sort of abstract holiness that makes him acutely dislikeable."

Farleigh's comment on this letter says a lot about Shaw's sharpness of perception: "The figure of Ecclesiastes *had* been taken from a frieze! I had omitted to turn the head towards the black girl—Shaw scored on this point, as he did on a good many other occasions; in fact, I discovered I was learning the business of illustration from the best master possible—a producer of plays, as well as author of them."

August was passing; Shaw, still in Malvern, wrote on the 29th of that month, his main theme the picture that depicts the Irishman trying to escape the clutches of Voltaire and the Black Girl: "[T]hough I am an execrable draughtsman I am a skilled and observant stage manager, always on the look-out for the right expression and movement. Keep me young, callow, fair, and scared out of my wits." Mohammed had to be as handsome as Farleigh could make him ("he was a princely genius"); Voltaire should be given a small implement to hold; and the Vanity Fair jury were all that could be desired, although the man with the moustache was very like some public man—he could not remember whom—but reckoned that he and Farleigh could chance his taking proceedings.

Farleigh sent the revised drawings of Voltaire, the "laborer in flight," and Christ at the well to Shaw. "These are now perfect," he said in response, except for one trifling alteration to the drawing of Christ at the well. "[T]he most troublesome of all in the book," Farleigh pronounced it, but Shaw liked the revision and was, as always, unstinting in his praise. "That has done the trick perfectly." He sent Farleigh £50 "to go on with."

"And so, it seemed, the book was finished," Farleigh wrote, almost regretfully. He sent his final account to Shaw, who responded promptly, on 24 September, raising Farleigh's figure to a round one, "as there may be some odd jobs to be done in concert with Maxwell—perhaps even a drawing for the postscript." A few comments on Farleigh's copyright and other business matters were followed by: "One fearful mistake has been discovered. Aircraftman Shaw, alias Colonel Lawrence, Prince of Damascus, etc., etc., who is among other things a keen book fancier, saw yesterday the set of proofs you sent me (many thanks) and highly approved of them, but made the devastating remark that no Arab ever sat with his legs crossed. We shall have to assume that Mahomet was an exception to all rules."

Time skipped by, and still Shaw failed to provide the promised afterword. On 17 October, by which time the book should have been in the book shops to catch the Christmas trade, Shaw wrote to Farleigh to tell him that going through the proofs, he felt the story did not have enough illustrations. It needed two more pictures: Pavlov sitting on the crocodile, and Micah with a flame shooting from his roaring mouth while the Black Girl and the lion fly for their lives. Farleigh had no option but to acquiesce; in fact, he says, he was pleased to get back on this particular job. This completed and referred to Shaw for approval, he had one more task: to provide an illustration for the afterword, which had been written at last. Following Shaw's suggestion, he drew bound volumes of books from the Bible and other likely (and unlikely) volumes: Job, Micah, Matthew, Mark, Luke, Writing Made Easy, Inge's Outspoken Essays, How to Spell and—horror!—Genisis (sic), which went out to the wide world, as though Shaw himself had sanctioned this orthographic liberty. Farleigh corrected his mistake as soon as he could. Some criticism of the two late entries, Pavlov and Micah, was followed by Shaw's approval of the revisions, and at last the book was ready.

Farleigh received a letter dated 13 November. "At last the book has gone to press," Shaw wrote. "It isn't half a bad job, is it? The girl makes a charming Leitmotif running through all the pictures. Anyhow, it's been a bit of fun. Is the enclosed all right for extra illustrations?"

There was more to be done before the book could be pronounced ready for the press—there always is—but Farleigh, working against the clock, had everything ready on time.

Seven months had passed since Shaw had told Kyllman about the "very blasphemous" pamphlet he had written, implying that he doubted its suitability for publication by Constable. Now, however, it was Constable as usual marketing the book, and Shaw telling Farleigh on 30 November that "Kyllman (Constable) reports that the first edition of 25,000 is already sold to the booksellers. He adds, 'Great excitement about John Farleigh.'"

The Adventures of the Black Girl in Her Search for God was published on 5 December 1932. The "first copy"—a prepublication copy—was given to T. E. Lawrence by Charlotte; the other 25,000 or so went out to the bookstores and were so in demand that five additional printings of the book in December alone became necessary, bringing the total to 57,000 copies. This highly un-Christmassy book was being gobbled up in the Christmas rush. From 1933 to 1936 there were nine more printings, totaling 48,000 copies. Meanwhile, in 1934, the tale was incorporated in *Short Stories, Scraps, and Shavings* in the *Standard Edition*; in 1946, for the Penguin edition, the title was shortened to *The Black Girl in Search of God and Some Lesser Tales* with the afterword transferred to the front as a preface. These changes were incorporated in the *Standard Edition* of 1947. There have been other publications of the tale since then, notably the corrected, definitive text brought out by Penguin under the editorial supervision of Dan H. Laurence in 1977 and the similarly revised text brought out in hardcover the same year by Viking in New York and in paperback by Penguin also in New York in *The Portable Bernard Shaw*, compiled and edited by Stanley Weintraub.

The first American edition of 6,400 copies was published on 24 February 1933 by Dodd, Mead, and Company. It missed Christmas and the probable sales windfall this would have brought but made up for this loss by being taken up as a dual selection by the Book-of-the-Month Club (its companion was *South Moon Under* by Marjorie Kinnan Rawlings); 47,000 copies of *The Black Girl* were on offer. Both Shaw and Farleigh disliked intensely the American edition. Farleigh wrote: "I hope America will forgive me if I say that her edition of the book was a travesty of the English edition." Shaw described it as a "counterfeit of [Maxwell's] work."[8]

As Shaw said to Farleigh, it had been a bit of fun; but now it was all over, or so they may have thought. It was in fact another beginning, for reaction to the book was widespread, and it ranged across the keyboard of human responses and went on for years. This is a story in itself.

1. "[I]f you study his wrinkles and nostrils you will see that they indicate a strong biting action." Shaw's rendering of Micah. Reproduced by permission of The Society of Authors, on behalf of the Bernard Shaw Estate.

2. "A dark man with wavy hair and a number six nose." Farleigh's rendering of
Micah. Reproduced by permission of The Society of Authors, on behalf of the Bernard Shaw Estate.

3. "I think the carrion bird was a mistake of mine." Shaw's rendering of "the myop" (Pavlov). Reproduced by permission of The Society of Authors, on behalf of the Bernard Shaw Estate.

4. "You are sitting on a sleeping crocodile." Farleigh has eliminated the carrion birds. Reproduced by permission of The Society of Authors, on behalf of the Bernard Shaw Estate.

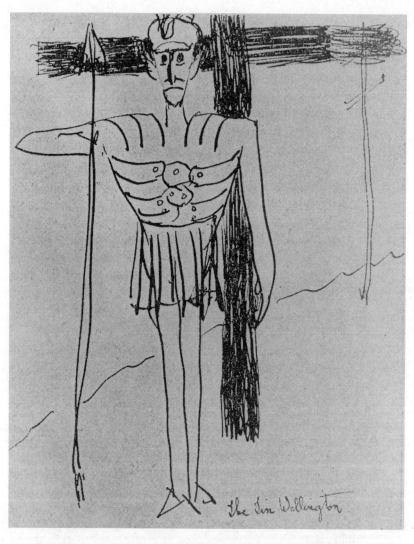

5. "My own drawings . . . suggest the pretentious futility of Cheltenham, not the
pride of Rome." Shaw's version of the Roman soldier. Reproduced by permission of
The Society of Authors, on behalf of the Bernard Shaw Estate.

6. "[H]e should be rigid, straight, inhuman, threatening." Farleigh's Roman soldier. Note the knobkerry, "like the sword of Damocles." Reproduced by permission of The Society of Authors, on behalf of the Bernard Shaw Estate.

7. Cover design for C. H. Maxwell's *Adventures of the White Girl in Her Search for God* (London: Lutterworth Press, 1933).

8. "You are nothing but a contradiction in terms." Title page of W. R. Matthews's
The Adventures of Gabriel in His Search for Mr Shaw (London: Hamish Hamilton,
1933).

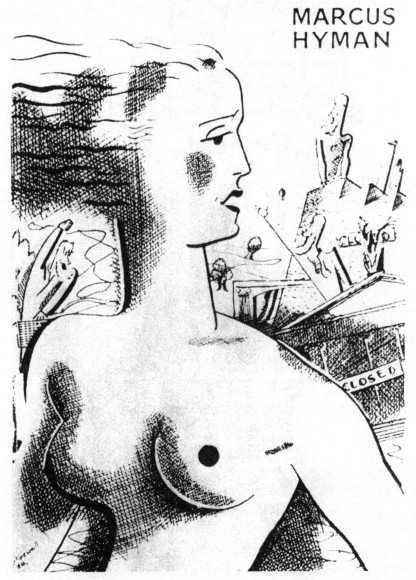

THE ADVENTURES OF THE WHITE
GIRL IN HER SEARCH FOR KNOWLEDGE

MARCUS
HYMAN

9. Cover design for Marcus Hyman's *The Adventures of the White Girl in Her Search for Knowledge* (London: Cranley, and Day, 1934).

10. "The man is a very sophisticated metropolitan critic, and not a raw youthful laborer." Shaw criticizing his version of the "laborer in flight." Reproduced by permission of The Society of Authors, on behalf of the Bernard Shaw Estate.

11. "Keep me young, callow, fair, and scared out of my wits." Farleigh does as required. Reproduced by permission of The Society of Authors, on behalf of the Bernard Shaw Estate.

Reaction, Censorship, Repudiation

I begin with the contributor who will soon leave this narrative—John Farleigh. Clever prepublicity had prepared the way for the intriguingly "different" book that would soon appear, but it was almost unnecessary in his case. It—he—was an instant success. "In two weeks," Farleigh wrote, "I had received sufficient offers of work to keep me busy for two years. Letters poured in; while the press poured out lavish praise."[1] He quotes (tongue in cheek) some of the remarks made by the critics about the Black Girl. "She was attractive" . . . "alluring" . . . "pleasing" . . . "delightful, but why nude?" . . . "[E]mbellished with exquisite engravings which depict a heroine remarkably bathykolpous and kallipygous." (For the uninitiated, "bathykolpous" means—to put it delicately— "deep-wombed," and "kallipygous" means "having a well-shaped bottom.") Of the many opinions voiced about the publication, the prize should go to the reviewer who described the product as a "pretty little picture book."

A psychological magazine reviewed this pretty little book and found much sexual symbolism, especially in the last engraving (Voltaire and the Black Girl preventing the Irishman from escaping), and wondered if Farleigh was aware of it. Considering that the issue at this point in the book is sexual—the Black Girl, a typical Shavian heroine, pursuing the man who was going to father her children—Farleigh could scarcely not have been aware of it. And of course there were letters to the press. Farleigh quotes one, from (of course) "Critical":

> I can understand the critics "sitting" on Mr Shaw for his recent book, but the way in which they have, with one exception, allowed Mr Farleigh's drawings to go unchallenged is another example of that simple and press-like innocence, or is it ignorance, the newspa-

per critics adopt towards all illustrated books—unless for some reason an art critic is brought in.

Mr Shaw shields himself behind his "inspiration," and to do him justice he did not intend to be *insolently* irreverent. Mr Farleigh was in no such mediumistic state when he illustrated the book, and is insolently irreverent whenever he is given the slightest chance. His conception of the Black Girl is physical rather than spiritual—she shows none of the tragedy of the black races, but more of the characteristics of an impertinent English girl who has been badly spoilt.

The Christ at the well is a dull Victorian conception, and the illustration showing the artist himself astride the cross, smoking a cigarette, is a clear indication of the artist's insolent attitude rather than the aloof one intended by the book.

I should be surprised if the illustrations have not done more harm than the text.

It is a pity the critics were not up to the other side of their job, when they could have harassed the artist as well as the author, so that they might enjoy a well deserved burning together.

"The most gratifying review, next to this letter," Farleigh goes on to remark, "was 'the pictures make the story clear to the blankest intelligence,' while the dizziest height of fame was reached when *Vogue*, in one of its reproductions of a fashionable woman, placed a copy of the book in her hand." Nearer home, a charming old lady, applying "Critical's" word to the deed, stopped short of getting Farleigh and Shaw burned at the stake but did publicly burn the book, while assorted clerics fulminated from their pulpits.

Looking back some thirty-plus years to the year in which he produced those drawings of the Black Girl, Farleigh blesses her while placing her firmly in his past: "I can never do *The Black Girl* again. . . . I have done better work since—though not so popular. Perhaps one has to be much better to be as popular again; perhaps popularity is not, after all, a question of quality, but something that may happen at any time to anyone." Perhaps so; but one should not forget what happened at a critical moment in his career, when a letter from the most famous writer in the world was dropped into his mailbox.

Farleigh's association with Shaw did not end here. He did other work with him, most notably the wood-engraved pictorial title page (repeated on the dust jacket) of the *Prefaces of Bernard Shaw*.[2] This ornate monumental design features an assortment of personalities (real and imaginary) in Shaw's career, including the Black Girl leaping from Shaw's head Athena-like; or is it a pictorial rendering of that "inspiration" Shaw made so much of? Or both?

There was a third contributor to this book, and in a sense he was the first: William Maxwell, the director of the printing house of R. and R. Clark. It was he who had suggested to Shaw that the story of the Black Girl could make an attractive publication if suitably illustrated, who had put Shaw in touch with Farleigh, and whose task it had become to oversee production. In theatrical terms, Maxwell was the stage manager, a brilliantly successful one at that. Yet, such is the nature of the stage manager's job—the printer's job, that is to say—he is ignored by the book reviewer and taken for granted by the public.

Fortunately he was noticed and afforded a lengthy appreciation in, appropriately, a trade journal. The article in the *Printing Trades Journal* was titled "Dressing Mr Shaw's Black Girl"; and the author, his name tucked away in an editorial aside on the contents page, was a Mr Olsson.[3] Gentlemen who pursued the printing trade were apparently shy of publicity.

But they knew and understood the ins and outs of their calling. It was only a month before, Olsson reminds his readers, that this journal had reviewed a work that had called on the expertise of several major talents, to wit a world-famous typographer, paper maker, and bookbinder, who had collaborated in producing a book that was sold to the public for twelve guineas. "The printer," Olsson remarks, "was only a trifle more important than the author and translator."

Twelve guineas. On the other hand: "This month we are proud to review a book, Shaw's *The Adventures of the Black Girl in Her Search for God*, produced in exemplary fashion and unique in certain forms of letterpress achievement, which yet has been turned out to sell in tens of thousands at two shillings and sixpence a copy." The inspiration and direction behind this achievement was the printer, Mr William Maxwell of R. and R. Clark of Edinburgh. How did he do it?

> He secured the illustrator Mr John Farleigh. . . . He introduced him to Shaw, persuaded him that illustrations were desirable (persuaded Shaw who had never had a single illustrated work produced

in his writing lifetime!), and having done so, created a rod for his own back by obtaining illustrations of such a superlative delicacy that their whole effect would have been lost without the most consummate care in the printing of the whole work.

Maxwell has surmounted what must be one of the most difficult book-production tasks of the year. Without conditioning the artist's work in any way, he has yet produced impressions as clear and flawless in the 50,000th copy as in the first.

Technical details follow. They are worth reviving after so long a silence, because the publication was an important event in printing terms, as much in Shaw's as in Farleigh's career. The paper of the first edition was Basingwerk parchment (sixpence a pound, Mr Olsson informs his readers, and cheaper in quantities), fixed and chosen by Maxwell as the kind that would please Shaw. It was supplied in quantities of double demy 80 lb sheets, the only modification, at Shaw's request, being that the usual deckle edge and watermark were to be omitted. "Beautiful paper," Olsson enthuses. But it presented a snag in that suitable ink had to be found because the matt surface of the paper did not readily pick up the full amount of ink deposited by the rollers on the plate. During the running a residue of ink was left; this gradually accumulated and entailed the cleaning of the inking apparatus three or four times a day. An ink of great density had to be used to display the fine detail of Farleigh's engraving against the solid black background.

The paper and ink problems solved, Maxwell and his staff in the process department and the machine room had to run the book off at a commercial speed while adhering to Maxwell's ideal of producing a book where none of the delicate line and stipple of the wood engraving would be damaged ("murdered," Olsson writes) by the electro printing, "these made from the original wood and soldered into electroplate," as Olsson puts it to his fellow technicians. "How well that trick was done the 50,000th copy shows."

What else had to be done? Maxwell did not resort to interleaving, which everyone else in the trade would have done. Instead he insisted on careful preparation by his best machine room experts, by using expensive ink and by running the printing at a slightly reduced speed.

And he worked closely with John Farleigh. Maxwell accorded him his due for the makeup of the pages, for Farleigh cut up the slip proofs sent him and pasted the illustrations in the positions he required. There was more to this than meets the eye, as Olsson goes on to relate, because to Farleigh fell the responsibility of the make-up of each and every page, down to the last detail. The finished book that went out to the bookstores was, in so far as it was a product in itself, the outcome of Maxwell's technical expertise and Farleigh's artistry.

Olsson then glances at a recent American publication of apparently similar impressive pedigree. "[A] very beautiful book, from one of the premier presses of America . . . practically a hand-made job, selling at almost museum prices." Tactful enquiries revealed that this book was the product of two processes, the blocks having been printed separately from the print by offset-litho.

Olsson cannot resist a superior smirk. "R. and R. Clark can give themselves a pat on the back for having achieved something for a half-crown public which one of the best American printers, working for dollar-laden bibliophiles, has failed to accomplish."

This reminds him of the story behind the selling price of *The Black Girl*. Maxwell wanted five shillings; Shaw wanted half that, two shillings and sixpence. Battle was joined, and Maxwell even enlisted the support of Charlotte Shaw. He brought his price down to four shillings. Shaw remained adamant. "The battle raged by conference and letter for several weeks. Closely typed pages of argument and pleading traveled from Edinburgh to the Parnassus in Whitehall Court and the Olympus in Hertfordshire. Six-worded denials, refusals and evasions went back on postcards."

Believing himself to have won after concluding his treaty with Charlotte, Maxwell took a few days off. It was an ill-advised rest, for in his absence from the office Shaw pulled the carpet from under his (and Charlotte's) feet by placing advertisements of the book at two shillings and sixpence. Olsson comments: "If G.B.S. was wise this time to let his printer do the printing (after the almost unreadable Blue Book clumsiness of the *Intelligent Woman's Guide to Socialism* for which he was solely responsible) he was wiser still not to listen to his printer's advice on selling prices."

In conclusion: "We must agree with Mr William Kermode, himself an experienced engraver for reproduction, who first drew our attention to this book, that it is definitely Mr Farleigh and Mr Maxwell who made it." These two could not have wished for a neater or better informed tribute than this. What about Shaw? Surely he should be featured as the author of a text that inspired the printer and the illustrator to outdo themselves? He does; and Olsson, swiftly transforming himself into a literary critic, has no time for him. Maxwell and Farleigh made the book, says he, one for reproducing such delicate work in such an enormous number of impressions, the other because his fancy enlivened a "boring and insipid treatise."

There one has it: a boring and insipid treatise. Having had his brief say, Olsson retreats to make way for Desmond MacCarthy's "penetrating continuation of Mr Shaw's inconclusive conclusion." This is how Olsson's tribute ends, then, with an excerpt from MacCarthy's review of the book. It is regrettable, because he and MacCarthy manage by their grudging coda to diminish Maxwell's and Farleigh's achievement.

On finishing the fable [MacCarthy wrote], I wanted to continue it in the manner of Voltaire. One day the Black Girl would discover a lump in her breast, which as time went on became more painful, until at last the torture became unbearable and it burst and stank. The bearded Irishman looking up from his spade, after examining the growth, would say, "undoubtedly you are suffering from one of the early experiments in the self-expression of the Life Force," and go on with his digging. And when, a year later, the old gentleman and the Irishman were disturbed at their gardening by a bomb which ruined the garden and blew off the former's leg, the latter would be able to offer his companion this consolation: "There is no reason for distress since the immanent Will must be triumphant. The Life Force, inspiring the destructive passions of politicians, has decided to scrap mankind and start again." At that moment his beard would be replaced by a full-bottomed wig, and the Irishman would turn before our eyes into our old friend Pangloss.[4]

MacCarthy had proved himself over the years as a most insightful critic of Shaw. His sensitive and penetrating observations on *Major Barbara* after its controversial premiere at the Royal Court Theatre in 1905 is a model of responsible criticism, for example. On that occasion the religious themes did not bother him; on the contrary, he recognized the work as primarily a play about religion—about religious passion and the conflict of two apparently irreconcilable faiths in one human breast—and had the courage to say so while most of his fellow critics were hysterically condemning it for its "blasphemies."[5] Here now, twenty-seven years later, this same critic was animadverting on *The Black Girl* as though personally affronted. To compound this, MacCarthy's remarks "in the manner of Voltaire" have nothing to do with the themes of the allegory (or "fable," as he calls it); they present Shaw's belief in a Life Force in a false light, and, worst lapse of all, the passage is badly written, lumps of lead next to the poised and pointed rhythms of Shaw's prose. One hopes MacCarthy came to regret this rush of blood and the haughty depreciation it prompted.

I return now to Shaw to consider first the critical response to his book. As the *New York Times* reported the day after publication, *The Black Girl* had a mixed reception in London, not a little of it hostile. The same mix of praise and denigration followed the book well into the new year. Some representative opinions follow.[6]

L.A.G. Strong in the *Spectator* of 9 December 1932 said that Shaw fell into the error of judging a belief by its silliest adherents and, while acknowledging that the allegory was vigorous and economical, thought that it finally lost momentum. R. Ellis Robert's review, "Shaw after Shaw," in the *New Statesman and Nation* of 10 December 1932 compared *The Black Girl* with *The Shewing-Up of Blanco Posnet,* in which the latter has the protagonist tracking down the soul while the former shows the soul in search of God. The ending is anticlimactic, for "Shaw, in the search for God, meets Bernard Shaw." Arvin Newton's obviously negative "Erin Go Blah" in the *New Republic* of 22 March 1933 reported that the tale said nothing profound and as art was vulgar and tedious, which was a view shared by Dorothea Brande in her "The Bishop of Everywhere's Bull" in the *American Review I* of April 1933: "very nearly Shaw at his worst," she wrote. Not surprisingly, the Christian press was forthright in its criticism, although W. E. Garrison in her "Shaw's Flight from God" in the *Christian Century* of 29 March 1933 is comparatively lenient. The book was irreverent, she thought, but it had a serious purpose in attacking church dogmatism, intolerance, and hypocrisy. "Whereas Shaw's black girl searches for God, Shaw himself seeks to escape God." The *Catholic World* of April 1933 gave the book short shrift: it was a fitting anticlimax to Shaw's career; it rambled, distorted, and lacked style. Shaw seemed to be moving toward madness, having become "not the thinking world's inspired clown but its tragic warning."

There was a more broad-minded response from the newspapers of record. Shaw, at seventy-six, was not likely to inflict quite the same high-voltage shock on its reviewers and readers as Shaw, at forty-six, had inflicted on the reviewers and readers of the same press in King Edward's day. The world had begun to catch up with him in some ways; one might almost say that to the reviewers of this press he was becoming "old hat," the gist of their response to *The Black Girl* being, "We have heard it before."[7] Even so, the (London) *Times* (and the *Times Literary Supplement* and the *New York Times*, in turn) found it perfectly possible, not merely to ignore the alleged "blasphemies" but to read into and appreciate Shaw's text as an enforcement of an evolutionary view of the Bible and an attempt to preserve its true spiritual values. Furthermore, "the keen ridicule pervading the account of the African savage girl's search for God among the representatives of the established creeds is directed neither against the proper Object of human worship nor against the founders of the great historical religions; but against the distorted ideas of these beings which have clouded the human mind and perverted the human will." Yes, perhaps the *Times*, soft-pedaling the issue, had heard it before but, its reviewer adds, "it is restated with incisive brilliance in this cameo story."

The reviewer for the *Times Literary Supplement* was handed a dual brief: to assess both Archibald Henderson's second "authorized" biography of Shaw, *Bernard Shaw: Playboy and Prophet*, and *The Black Girl* in one article. This is how he sets about his task:

> Mr Shaw is accused by his critics of a taste for *longueurs;* and it may be that some of his last acts bear out this charge. Yet he is the man who has just published in the form of an apologue a critique of the chief world religions that extracts the essentials in about seventy pages; and he is the man who told us all we need to know about his personal history in a Preface to his recently published first novel, "Immaturity," which is one of the autobiographical gems of our language—and which occupies exactly forty-four pages of print. This makes us wonder what he can really think of the eight hundred and fifty pages odd of Mr Henderson's "authorized" biography.

Whatever Shaw may have thought of Henderson's book, it is plain the reviewer thinks it terrible, and he devotes three-quarters of a column to telling one why. I latch on to some of the following acerbic phrases, not to put Henderson down again, but to highlight the vividness with which

Shaw the original emerges alongside Henderson's drab and remote secondhand image: "at a loss to understand [Henderson's] principles of selection . . . Shaw's life, his works and the reaction of critics to these are
confusedly contained in the book . . . biographical material is jejune and
sloppy . . . an industrious if disorderly compilation of facts . . . that it is
fully 'authorized,' destined to rank as the definitive portrait of its subject
we must take leave to doubt."[8]

Focus shifts from Henderson to Shaw, and it is like stepping from ditch
water into a crystalline stream: "Mr Shaw's new religious fable . . . does
not mark a step forward in [his] religious thought, but is rather a dazzling
and incisive exposure of current religious errors (or what its author holds
to be such) in the light of those well-known maxims of the Life Force,
creative evolution and the slow self-perfection of the Deity through human ascent which Mr Shaw has preached for many years."

The reviewer then follows the Black Girl in her search, pausing now
and again to highlight and typify an encounter he has found particularly
telling. For example, the three-cornered duel involving the Arab, the image maker, and the Black Girl is like a scene from one of the liveliest of the
Shaw comedies; and the chattering caravan of curious whites damn
themselves by their inadequacies in wanting to shoot the Black Girl for
finding her too beautiful and brainy. This review, necessarily brief because of the space occupied by Henderson, concludes:

> We doubt if this delightful little fantasy needed an explanation; but
> who could hope to persuade Mr Shaw that explanation is ever su-
> perfluous? And perhaps some readers will be reassured by the con-
> cluding essay pointing out the proper way to use the Bible, which is
> neither to "boot it into the dustbin," as the Soviet has done, nor to
> allow its admixture of primitive superstition to discredit its value as
> the record of a progressively spiritualized religion. There is nothing
> sensationally new in this message "at the present world crisis" from
> the "sort of unofficial Bishop of Everywhere" that Mr Shaw claims
> to be. Quite a number of properly lawn-sleeved Bishops could swal-
> low most of it—so the Black Girl may go on peacefully weeding her
> garden.[9]

It is a neat and graceful tribute, and another reminder of the high, virtu-
ally unassailable position Shaw had achieved by the 1930s, in spite of the
"perverse" incursions he was making into international politics at the

time. That is another story; the point about this story of the Black Girl is that he (and his heroine) struck a note that resonated round the world, as I will show.

The *New York Times* reviewed *The Black Girl* two-and-a-half months later when the American edition appeared and praised the "parable" as a "compact and biting satire calculated to provoke as much furious discussion as any dramatic work from [Shaw's] nimble pen"—those most certain to be provoked being the cocksure fundamentalist and the cocksure scientist.[10] "As is always the case with Shaw," the reviewer continues, "there is genuine seriousness behind the buffoonery, of which there is not a little." Buffoonery? Perhaps it would be nearer the mark to see many of the confrontations and cameos that comprise *The Black Girl* as utterly serious fantasy shot through with humor. (As Shaw would say to Dame Laurentia McLachlan, "Why should the devil have all the fun?") The reviewer's mild rebuke is balanced by a mild tribute: "But Mr. Shaw's conception of what the Bible really is will hardly satisfy those who have found in it profounder values than he is ready to perceive. He can, on occasion, stoop to cheap flippancy . . . [and] it is in the concluding episode of the black girl's search that the buffoonery reaches its highest pitch, and, at the same time, that Shaw assumes his most serious and sincerest attitude."

Like his peers in the two London papers cited above, the reviewer observes that Shaw's quarrel is not with the Bible itself but with people who misread and misapply it. This must, one feels, be obvious to any sensible person, yet it is surprising how many sensible people failed to see this and took profound umbrage at what they read as Shaw's attack on the Bible. A few of these people, and a few institutions managed by such people, may now be brought before the bar of history and, notwithstanding the *Times*'s comment that properly lawn-sleeved bishops need lose no sleep over the book, one of them did; indeed, more than one cleric did. The first to be quoted in the press was the bishop of Winchester, the Right Reverend Cyril Garbett, whose letter in the *Diocesan Chronicle* was reported in the *New York Times*.[11] "We have a real cause of complaint," Bishop Garbett wrote, "against brilliant writers like Shaw who attack Christianity as set forth by its weakest, not its strongest, exponents or who label a construction of their own ignorance on Christianity and then show how easily they can destroy it." Shaw is not mentioned again, but one feels that his disquieting—his disruptive—presence continues to hover over the doom-laden vision of a world in religious turmoil conjured up in the remainder of the bishop's letter.

Thus did Garbett set the ball rolling, and once given this not inordinately powerful shove, it has been kept going down the corridor of the years by an amazing variety of persons. Some have been pro-Shaw and his Black Girl, like Brigid Brophy; one or two have been satirical; many have been anti-Shaw—like Dr G.E.J. Greene, who instigated what may be described as the affair of the County Wexford Bee-Keepers' Association. It was a trivial affair, yet its bizarreness made it newsworthy and grist to the mills of the world press. The Wexford Bee-keepers' Association was, as Shaw told his Polish translator, Floryan Sobieniowski, "a harmless little Irish society of village honey sellers,"[12] and at its meeting of 29 December 1932 (three weeks after publication of *The Black Girl*), Dr Greene proposed that Shaw's name be dropped from the list of life members because of the blasphemies perpetrated in that book. "A man who made observations that struck with sarcastic ridicule at the very foundations of Christianity should not be associated even remotely with their society," said Dr Greene.[13] He was seconded by a Mr McDonald who did not wish to be associated with an infidel. The meeting decided to postpone the issue to the Annual General Meeting in late January 1933. As the *Times* neutrally reported this occasion: "There was on the agenda of the annual meeting of the Co. Wexford Beekeepers' Association in Enniscorthy yesterday a resolution which had been proposed by Dr Greene, and adjourned from a previous meeting, that Mr George Bernard Shaw's name be removed from the list of life members in consequence of what were described as 'blasphemous statements' in his book 'The Adventures of the Black Girl in her Search for God.' On a show of hands the meeting decided not to hear Dr Greene."[14]

Vegetarian, sweet-toothed Shaw liked honey; even so this life membership of the Wexford Bee-Keepers' Association seems weird—"for a reason which passes all understanding," as St John Ervine comments[15]—until one reads in the letter to Sobieniowski that Shaw had once given the association a donation of a few guineas. In any event, those beekeepers, sensible fellows, kept faith with their famous life member and performed a perfect squelch on disagreeable Dr Greene, which did not prevent the usual cohorts of inexact journalists from broadcasting round the world that the beekeepers had expelled Shaw.

One moves on to 3 February 1933 and reads in the *Times* that the

"Cambridge Town Council upheld yesterday by a large majority a decision of its library committee to ban from the public library Mr Bernard Shaw's book, 'The Adventures of the Black Girl in Her Search for God.'" And on to 23 March of the same year, when the same paper reported on the meeting of the Education Committee of the London County Council, which had considered the requisition list of the teachers' library at County Hall from which Shaw's book had been pointedly excluded.

> Mrs DRAKE (Labour) protested against the exclusion. . . . The note by which the book was refused stated "not at present—later on, when it has passed the stage of the book of the day, it may be reconsidered." If it meant anything at all, said Mrs Drake, it meant that when the book became a classic and the teachers no longer wished to read it, it would be placed on the list. (Laughter) She did not suppose it was Mr Bernard Shaw's best work, but it was written in all sincerity.
>
> The REV. A. G. PRICHARD said that he did not believe in anything in the nature of an Index Expurgatorius with regard to books. He thought it unfortunate that the committee should exercise any such powers; but if there was any book of Mr Bernard Shaw's which should be excluded he thought the committee had chosen wisely. The work did not show Mr Bernard Shaw at his best, and was offensive to some people.
>
> The CHAIRMAN of the Sub-committee said that the committee had a limited amount of money, and had to exercise a choice. Here was a book of doubtful morals. It was submitted to the Chief Inspector, who said that in his opinion it was not wise to place it on the requisition list at present.
>
> The report was received.

One may spare a passing thought on the effect a half-crown book could have on a library budget, no matter how limited; also on the Reverend Prichard's cerebral feat in being both broad-minded and narrow-minded at one and the same time. But the ways of education committees and library subcommittees are not for ordinary mortals to unravel, and out of the window *The Black Girl* went.

Private reactions by friends to whom Shaw would have sent the book suggest that on the whole, if their silence is anything to go by, they were unmoved. There were one or two exceptions. Sydney Olivier was one.

Shaw's friend since the early Fabian days, a former senior official of the Colonial Office and governor of Jamaica, he responded at length because the Black Girl's background and situation reminded him of the situation he had encountered in the West Indies, Jamaica in particular. He thought Shaw's lady missionary a caricature but recognized qualities in her that he had encountered in Jamaica, specifically the tendency of missionaries to become slightly bigoted evangelical fundamentalists. He had just completed a book himself to counteract this teaching, was intending to send it to a club of young Jamaicans, and: "I am hesitating whether also to send them a copy of *The Black Girl*." As for the political-economic subtext of Shaw's book, he commented with feeling on the failure of the colonial government and white employers to recognize the fact that the laborers were "really *very* poor and suffer hardship from poverty, and what they manage to produce for themselves and are satisfied with, costs them physical and intellectual labor of which any white man would be simply incapable under similar conditions." He cites the Black Girl's comment, made during her confrontation with the Caravan of the Curious, that it is impossible to get Europeans to understand what is "less than enough" for Africans—"a thing I have been up against all my life." And yet the only people capable of appreciating the black man's economic plight were the missionaries, "who believe they can only give the black man what he wants by means of their fundamentalist formulas." There spoke one of the original "Three Musketeers" of the Fabian Society, and Shaw (D'Artagnan of the group) would have been in full accord with the sentiments; he had in fact already incorporated them in the Black Girl's diatribe against white exploitation of blacks.

Olivier thought the Black Girl "in her full dress charming" and "ought to be influential as a mild diaphoretic"—that is to say, in inducing perspiration in the beholder. He chided Shaw for describing the writer of the Book of Revelations as a "drug-addict." A "blunder," he said, for John of Patmos was no drug addict but a mystical symbolist in the line of Blake.[16]

Beatrice Webb confided her opinion to her diary; she often did where Shaw was concerned, often carpingly, sometimes all sweetness and light. She is both here, combining her remarks on what she regarded as a very poor lecture by Shaw at the Kingsway Hall ("a painfully incoherent tirade about nothing in particular, except for the laudation of Oswald Mosley as the 'man of the future'!") with praise of *The Black Girl*:

As against the Kingsway failure, there is the little brochure, beautifully illustrated, *The Black Girl*, price 2s 6d, with its epilogue on the evolution and the present state of religion, which is brilliant. If it were not for the author's prestige it would be considered blasphemous by all churchmen, conventional and otherwise. . . .

I have watched for reviews of GBS's deadly dart—disguised as a fascinating Xmas card—and note with interest that only Gerald Gould takes our view of its potency; otherwise the reviewers have wittingly or unwittingly dismissed it as one more *jeu d'esprit* from the G.O.M. of literature; *The Times* even politely suggested that it conformed to the canon of fashionable 'modernism' in Christian exegesis. I still think, with Gould, that this 2s 6d illustrated tract for the times is perhaps the most effective single publication of GBS's wit and wisdom so far as the mass of readers, especially young readers, are concerned.[17]

There one has it again: Shaw's "deadly dart" would be considered "blasphemous," and this assessment comes from a moderately objective source.

Here I will digress to consider the question of blasphemy, bearing in mind that Shaw himself—anticipating Beatrice Webb by several months—described his "pamphlet" to Dame Laurentia McLachlan and others by this term, telling her in his letter of 12 [14] April that it was "absolutely blasphemous, as it goes beyond all the churches and all the gods." A postscript adds that the story is "very irreverent and iconoclastic."

Shaw, if he was being blasphemous, stood in an illustrious line of blasphemers: Jesus was regarded as one in his claim to be the Son of God, also in the attribution of his authority over demons; Paul was regarded as a blasphemer before his conversion. Since then, and over many centuries, blasphemy—perceived as a threat to the solidarity of the church—was regarded as the word of the Antichrist and repressed accordingly. However, definitions of this sin have been modified over the years, particularly since the Enlightenment, when secular political authority began to subdue the power of the church. Even so, as recently as the 1930s, blasphemy continued to loom large in all major world religions as a heinous sin.

Shaw would have been aware of all this. He never used words loosely, and here his designation of his work as "blasphemous" is in strict keeping with the definition found in any authoritative work of reference: contemptuous or abusive language about God, irreverent talk about or treatment of a religious or sacred thing. The Bible is unambiguous in prescribing the punishment to be meted out to anyone who commits this sin; Leviticus 24.16 lays down the law: "[H]e that blasphemeth the name of the Lord shall surely be put to death, and all the congregation shall stone him." If Shaw did not qualify to be stoned or burned at the stake in 1932, as he would have five or six hundred years before, his "blasphemies" could still have been regarded as a crime in church law and in common law as well, although the term "blasphemy," now secularized, describes a sin not against God but against society and is seen as applicable when scurrilous attacks on the Deity offend believers or cause a breach of the peace. So it is still a crime, though not a capital one, in Britain and some other nominally Christian countries, while in Islamic states a considerably more rigorous attitude applies, as witness the *fatwa* (decree by an Islamic religious leader) in Iran against Salman Rushdie. So Shaw could have been charged and brought before a court by, for example, the old lady who publicly burned the book, and *The Black Girl* could therefore have been seen to be "absolutely blasphemous" theologically speaking and potentially blasphemous in common law. Dr Greene of Wexford had a case.

It is apropos to set *The Black Girl* up against the decrees governing the prohibition of publications as defined in the Roman Catholic *Index Expurgatorius*, bearing in mind that Shaw's principal focus in his designation of the work as "blasphemous" was a Benedictine nun to whom the edicts of the church would have been absolute. These decrees are: "Books defending heresies, i.e. doctrines contrary to divine revelation . . . Books derogatory to God, the Blessed Virgin, the Saints . . . Books vilifying the sacraments, the clerical or religious state, the hierarchy, the Church. . . . Books professedly treating of, narrating or teaching lewdness and obscenity. . . . Books teaching or recommending sorcery, spiritism, Christian Science, or other superstitions. . . . Books defending as lawful or harmless, Freemasonry, divorce, Socialism, suicide, dueling."[18]

From what one reads here, *The Black Girl* was heretical in the highest degree on more than one count. In fact, it was not listed in the *Index;*

neither was any of Shaw's other publications. But his prepublication anxiety seems to have been well founded, more so if one considers his comment to Farleigh in one of his early letters (that of 24 May 1932, in which he discusses the business side of their association) that a German illustrator, whom "the Germans" wanted him to use, had been imprisoned for blasphemy. This illustrator "richly deserved [imprisonment] for his hideously clever work," he tells Farleigh. "We must show them how it is to be done." If this says anything, it is that Shaw was tactfully advising Farleigh not to overstep the mark.

One may indulge in surmise that Shaw, recognizing the problem, was genuinely anxious about the kind of reception his "pamphlet" would be accorded by the press, the Christian church, and the public at large; and, afraid that the "crimes" committed in the text would outrage religious sensibilities, agreed to publication only when he saw the opportunity to dress his "blasphemies" up in a Farleigh-esque Christmas package—thus, in the not unusual Shavian way, festooning an uncompromising text with lashings of exotic distractions. One may recall again the cries of "blasphemy!" that rent the critical air when *Major Barbara* was produced and also the ban imposed on stage performances of *The Shewing-Up of Blanco Posnet* and be certain that Shaw had no wish to endure yet again the controversies that ensued in each case, least of all in a court of law confronting a synod of vengeful bishops. This may seem mere fancy, and it probably is: no "fascinating Xmas card" has ever been known to cause a breach of the peace. Beatrice Webb was right: Shaw's immense prestige was proof against any public charge of blasphemy, while Farleigh, settled within this Shavian umbrella, was similarly protected.

A further consideration is the manner of the utterance rather than the content. Dr Greene thought Shaw's utterance ill-mannered—irreverent, that is—and thus blasphemous; his beekeeping cronies disagreed, finding its author liable for neither prosecution nor, worse, expulsion from their association. "Manner" and the linked question of irreverence (or profanity) is plainly a matter of personal response, and arguably most of the hundreds of thousands of people who read the book in the 1930s or have done so since, if pressed for an answer, would have seen it as possibly blasphemous but not outrageously so and—given the temper of the more resilient postwar years—as a timely adjuration to allow a breath of skepticism into the stale confines of age-old sanctities. As the reviewer for the

Times said, "the keen ridicule pervading the account of the African savage girl's search . . . is directed . . . against the distorted ideas of these beings which have clouded the human mind and perverted the human will." Most readers probably saw *The Black Girl* in this way.

There were, however, two emphatic rejections. Both were comparatively small in themselves, yet they were not negligible, reflecting as they did deep-rooted objections to the book. The first occurred in Ireland, where on 1 May 1933, the Irish Censorship Board prohibited sale and circulation of *The Black Girl*. The second rejection was from Shaw's friend, Dame Laurentia McLachlan, abbess of Stanbrook Abbey. I will consider each in turn.

It was six months after publication of *The Black Girl* that the Irish censors suppressed its sale and circulation. It is number 307 in the Register of Prohibited Publications, its less than exalted companions being such works as *The Adventures of a Coquette* by one Gaston Leroux, and *All About Jane* by Pamela Wynne; also, at a possibly more exalted level, *All Men Are Enemies* by Richard Aldington. One fairly unbiased commentator has said that prohibitions in Ireland "sometimes bordered on the ludicrous,"[19] and as far as the *Times* and the *New York Times* were concerned, the banning of *The Black Girl* was a nonevent, such an action being all too predictable in Ireland and not considered worth reporting. Shaw himself took the ban calmly, even though some years before, when the Censorship of Publications Act of 1929 was being debated in the Dàil (the Irish parliament), he had published a sarcastic letter on the intended legislation in the London *Time and Tide* (16 November 1928) and the Dublin *Irish Statesman* (17 November 1928). By 1933, however, finding himself proscribed, he refused to become excited partly because—as he ingenuously told Sobieniowski in his letter of 24 July 1933—the ban was imposed too late to injure sales of the book in Ireland, and also because he was too experienced and disillusioned a campaigner to think there was anything one could do to reverse the decision.

W. B. Yeats, on the other hand, was not prepared to take things lying down. Perhaps he hoped to repeat the victory of 1909, when he and Lady Gregory (mainly Lady Gregory) had confronted the Lord Lieutenant of Ireland and forced him to rescind the banning of *The Shewing-Up of Blanco Posnet* when the play, refused a license in England, was scheduled for production at the Abbey Theatre. But Lady Gregory, who had died some months before, in 1932, was not there to add her forceful personality to a confrontation with government, and it was through the Irish Academy of Letters that Yeats intended to act.

This academy—founded the year before with Yeats the driving force behind it and Shaw, advising him from England, an unwilling first president—was set up primarily to promote serious literature and resist literary censorship in Ireland, controlled as this was by Roman Catholic clerics. Membership included a number of Irish literary luminaries, and although James Joyce and Sean O'Casey declined nomination, all in all it amounted to a considerable intellectual pressure group, to the extent that men and women of letters can be accounted a "pressure group" when confronting government. Moreover, two Nobel laureates—Yeats and Shaw—were of their number, and Yeats was a former senator in the Irish parliament, factors that one might have thought would cause the minister of justice and nominal boss of the Censorship Board, one Patrick Ruttledge, to have second thoughts.

He had no second thoughts; he prevaricated instead, telling the deputation from the academy (apparently a one-person "deputation," the academy secretary, Higgins) that he had read *The Black Girl* and could himself see no reason for its banning and promising to take the matter up with the Censorship Board. One wonders how strongly he urged the board to reconsider its decision, how strenuously he queried its designation of *The Black Girl* as "in its general tendency indecent and obscene." All that the academy subsequently learned in a letter from Ruttledge was that he had after full consideration decided not to revoke the prohibition. As Dan H. Laurence relates, "When the Academy demanded to know the reason for this ban, it was informed by Ruttledge . . . that it was not usual for the Ministry to offer reasons for the banning of any book other than those given in the official gazette."[20]

Yeats would not accept this and considered legal action, but Shaw dissuaded him. "You can't prosecute a Government: the King can do no wrong," he declared, telling Yeats that any recourse to the courts by whomever would be sure to end in defeat. Then, recalling no doubt his own "Miltonic essay" written in 1909 for the benefit of the parliamentary subcommittee appointed to look into stage censorship—an essay that the committee summarily rejected—he went on to enlighten Yeats on the impossibility of getting a government to budge by enlightened argument. As he pointed out: "You say that the Academy cannot leave the matter where it is; but what can it do? When the *force majeure* is on the other side it is the greatest of mistakes to attempt any sort of compulsion. Articles and Miltonic essays may be hurled at the government if the editors and publishers can be induced to print them: that is all. And even that will be a waste of time. I shall not protest: if the Churchmen think my book subversive they are quite right from their point of view."[21]

Yeats reluctantly allowed the matter to drop, and from then on the Republic of Ireland had to survive without benefit of *The Black Girl* in its bookstores and libraries.

All this is confirmed and amplified—and given a slightly different slant—in a reminiscence by Mervyn Wall, who relates that he was told about the confrontation between the academy and the Censorship Board by the poet F. R. Higgins:

> When Shaw's *The Black Girl in Her Search for God* was banned by our censorship board, Higgins was secretary of the newly-founded Irish Academy of Letters, of which Yeats had persuaded an unwilling Shaw to accept the presidency. Shaw's novel had not an obscene word in it, but had been banned because of illustrations of a black woman wandering nude through a forest.
>
> Higgins went to see his friend Ruttledge, Minister for Justice, who admitted that the Censorship Board had exceeded its powers. It had only legal power to ban on account of the printed word, not because of illustrations.
>
> Ruttledge, pleading old friendship, begged Higgins not to pursue the matter further because of the embarrassment it would cause the government, but Higgins wrote immediately to Shaw urging him to take action in the courts, and thus show up the irresponsibility and absurdity of the Censorship Board. Higgins then drew a postcard from his pocket and showed me Shaw's reply: *What's the use of throwing stones at the devil? G.B.S.*"[22]

Shaw was quite right: it was the strong clerical element on the Censorship Board that urged suppression of the book, and it was apparently Farleigh's depiction of a nude Black Girl (with Shaw's concurrence) that prompted the words "indecent and obscene" to be applied in the official prohibition. As he said in his letter to Yeats: "Only, as the word obscene can hardly be applied to my text, I wish some member of the Dail would ask Mr Ruttledge whether, if I issue a special edition for Ireland with the negress depicted in long skirts, the ban will be withdrawn."

This may miss the point, which is that the clerics would, if they could, have found against the book by one or more of the criteria laid down by the decrees defining heresy. Not able to do this because of the terms of the legislation—which specified "indecent and obscene" as the sole criterion on which they could act—they had to resort to that term, surely the flabbiest and most inaccurate of designations for *The Black Girl*. Shaw saw through it all immediately; so did everyone else with an ounce of common sense.

The other quarrel, with Dame Laurentia McLachlan, was much more serious as far as Shaw was concerned.

She was born Margaret McLachlan. At the age of eighteen, on 5 September 1884 (the same day Shaw joined the Fabian Society), she was admitted as a novice to the closed Order of Benedictines at Stanbrook Abbey, a Victorian Gothic pile (as "A Nun of Stanbrook" describes it) on the outskirts of the village of Callow End, four miles from Worcester and on the road to Malvern, the venue for the Annual Theatre Festival at which, from 1929, many of Shaw's plays were given their initial "provincial" outing.[23] Laurentia McLachlan (Sister Laurentia) would remain at Stanbrook for the rest of her life, rising in the order to become prioress and, in 1931, abbess. She was highly intelligent and well read, though perhaps within a comparatively restricted field. In spite of the physically confined nature of her vocation, she was so "without frontiers" that she became well known among cognoscenti as an authority on plainsong and liturgical music. That she and Shaw should become friends, considering the different worlds they inhabited, exceeds the bounds of probability, but friends they became, bonded by spiritual affinity as much as intellectual acumen. Bonded as well—as Sydney Cockerell noted and Michael Holroyd has demonstrated—by the fact that they seemed paradoxically to complement each other's nature.[24]

It was Shaw's old friend Sydney Cockerell who brought them together. He and Cockerell came to know each other in the 1880s, when Cockerell was William Morris's secretary at the Kelmscott Press. The early acquaintance grew into friendship when they formed part of a group that toured the Continent—Italy in particular—in 1885, and thereafter they remained close, or as close as a compulsively busy play-wright–man-of-affairs and a somewhat reclusive antiquarian (subsequently director of the Fitzwilliam Museum in Cambridge) could become. Shaw respected and admired him to the extent that he nominated Cockerell his literary executor in his will.

Cockerell came to know Dame Laurentia in 1907, when he visited Stanbrook Abbey to examine a thirteenth-century psalter; he soon became an adviser to the Stanbrook Abbey Press. Impressed by Dame Laurentia's "beautiful voice" as well as her deserved reputation as a scholar—fascinated also by conversing through a double grille on matters of mutual bibliophilic interest—he attempted tentatively to introduce her to contemporary literature and ideas. Tolstoy was a failure; Dame Laurentia dismissed him firmly as someone whose works were not at all on the lines in which her reading lay. What, then, about Bernard Shaw? "I wonder whether G.B.S.'s fame has got as far as Stanbrook," he asked in 1907, "and whether he is there regarded as an imp of the devil—I have known him for many years and regard him not only as one of the cleverest (that is nothing) but as one of the best and honestest of living Englishmen." This elicited another uncompromising response: "I have never heard of Mr Bernard Shaw. . . . I don't like to think that a person whom you regard with respect should be to us as a limb of the evil one!" Thus dismissed, Shaw (through Cockerell) had to bide his time.

This came seventeen years later, the enquiry coming not from Cockerell but Dame Laurentia herself. She had heard about Shaw's new play, *Saint Joan,* and was interested in it. Cockerell leaped at the opportunity offered him. He would lend her his special copy, he told her, "special" because the play had not yet been published. She read it and was pleased with it, though critical of certain aspects. Cockerell wasted no time; Shaw and Charlotte, urged by Cockerell, called on Dame Laurentia on the afternoon of 24 April 1924. It was not, it would seem, a particularly auspicious meeting (Dame Laurentia was reticent about it in her letter to Cockerell), but sufficient goodwill was generated for Charlotte to admit to him that she and G.B.S. had liked her *very much.* Charlotte's visits to Stanbrook gradually fell away, but Shaw called again and again, and they wrote to each other regularly. So gradually through the 1920s and into the early 1930s the friendship grew. Charlotte regarded his visits as a kind of flirtation, but Cockerell, accompanying Shaw on one visit, observed that he had never seen him so abashed by anyone but William Morris. It was as though he admitted to being in the presence of a being superior to himself and was on his best behavior.[25]

It was, on the face of it, an unlikely match: on the one hand, a world-famous playwright and man of affairs, a notorious freethinker in religious, not to say other, more worldly, matters; and on the other hand, a nun whose cloistered existence had shut her off from the hurly-burly of the world—Shaw's world—for fifty years. Yet there was a matching of minds, particularly in matters metaphysical and spiritual, and it is in this that one may detect a motive in each for maintaining the friendship. Shaw's was perhaps the more disinterested in that it began and ended in the enjoyment and intellectual stimulation he derived from conversing with Laurentia on matters that, supremely important to him, were shrugged off by the outside world. Her interest, apart from a like enjoyment and stimulation, included a declared mission to bring Shaw to salvation. As she put it: "[W]hen he found that whatever I am is the result of my life here he was impressed. This gives me confidence to hope that God may use me for this soul's salvation. If it were only a matter of his liking me I should think little of it, but it seems that life here, and therefore the Church does attract him. God give me grace to help this poor wanderer so richly gifted by you."

The poor wanderer had other thoughts on the subject.

It is not necessary to pursue their correspondence through the 1920s and early 1930s. Suffice it to say that by the end of the 1920s, Shaw and Dame Laurentia were—if not exactly billing and cooing through that double grille—extraordinarily close. The friendship reached its apogee in 1931, when Shaw and Charlotte visited the Holy Land, and Shaw picked up two little stones in Bethlehem, "one to be thrown blindfold among the others in Stanbrook garden so that there may always be a stone from Bethlehem there . . . and the other for your own self." Shaw had the second stone mounted as a personal memento for Dame Laurentia. "[A]n exquisite example of the silversmith's art," says the Nun of Stanbrook. Dame Laurentia was enchanted. This was in October 1931. Four months later in Knysna, Shaw wrote *The Black Girl*.

"Your letter has given me a terrible fright. . . . I forgot all about you, or I should never have dared," Shaw told Laurentia in his letter of 12 [14] April 1932, where he tells her about his "pamphlet" and relates the plot to her.[26] This is a smiling brazen lie: Shaw could not possibly have forgot-

ten all about Dame Laurentia, and neither would he "never have dared."
That he wrote to her shortly after his return to London, telling her that
he had written a booklet that could conceivably upset her, indicates that
she would have been in his thoughts even in distant Knysna, more so
when working on his "absolutely blasphemous" "pamphlet." And her
reaction, which appears to have consisted in asking some direct questions,
probably did give him a "terrible fright."

As for his not daring to write such a work, he would surely have come
to see that Dame Laurentia had been trying by sundry subtle and perhaps
not-so-subtle means to shepherd the "poor wanderer" into the Catholic
fold. *The Black Girl* was his response, his declaration to Dame Laurentia
and other proselytizers, Catholic and otherwise—such as Father Vassall-
Phillips and Mabel Shaw—that he, Shaw, would dare to assert his independence of mind and spirit in all matters, religious as well as secular, no
matter what the opposition (or anger) it provoked.

I have discussed the correspondence that followed immediately on
Shaw's "confession" to Dame Laurentia—that, having read the printed
text Shaw sent her (with the inscription about the "Inspiration" that produced it), she admitted to agreeing with many of his ideas but said she
would never forgive him were he to publish the work. Shaw followed this
up with a scrap of "heavenly" dialogue featuring God and the Angel
Gabriel that she took to imply, with fairly good cause, that Shaw had
abandoned the idea of publishing. As she fondly put it, her dear Brother
Bernard was going to be good about it, and she felt light and springy
again.

A Nun of Stanbrook surmises that Dame Laurentia's letters during
the course of 1932—while the text was being prepared for publication—
indicated that Shaw would no longer be persona grata at Stanbrook if it
were published. Undeterred, Shaw sent her a copy soon after publication
with this brief, slightly squirming inscription dated 14 December 1932:[27]
"Dear Sister Laurentia[:] This black girl has broken out in spite of everything. I was afraid to present myself at Stanbrook in September. Forgive
me, G. Bernard Shaw."

Shaw was not going to hide his "sin" from his most severe critic. She,
in turn, was not prepared to allow him to escape from the consequences
of his transgression. She reacted at once with a letter that reproved Shaw
vigorously for publishing the book. He and Charlotte had already left
England for a world cruise aboard RMS *Empress of Britain*, which they

boarded in Monaco on 16 December, and her letter followed him to the Far East, where it reached him, months later, in Bangkok. Her words plainly caused him to think long and hard before attempting a rejoinder. He had, he told her in the letter that was eventually sent off, torn up his first letter because he felt it might wound her again; then he had written another, which he had also torn up for the same reason; and then the notebook in which he had written a third letter in shorthand for the ship's stenographer to transcribe had been stolen from his deck chair. The outcome of these setbacks was the fourth letter of 29 June, in which Shaw seems to be trying with characteristic blarney to put the disagreement behind them:

> I was ridiculously surprised at your reception of The Black Girl story, which I innocently took to be a valuable contribution to the purification of religion from horrible old Jewish superstitions; and even my callousness was pierced by finding that it had shocked and distressed you. . . .
>
> I will not try to reproduce the letter: the moment has passed for that. Besides, I am afraid of upsetting your faith, which is still entangled in those old stories which unluckily got scribbled up on the Rock of Ages before you landed there. So I must go delicately with you, though you need have no such tenderness with me; for you can knock all the story books in the world into a cocked hat without shaking an iota of *my* faith.
>
> Now that I think of it, it was a venial sin to write me such a cruel letter; and I think you ought to impose on yourself the penance of reading The Black Girl once a month for a year. I have a sneaking hope that it might not seem so very wicked the tenth or the eleventh time as you thought it at first. You must forgive its superficial levity. Why should the devil have all the fun as well as all the good tunes?[28]

But the blarney did not work, still less the protestation of "innocence." This was not the kind of disagreement Laurentia could put behind her. She wrote back: "Thank you for your letter which explains your silence. The fate of your long letter is very sad, but if I may judge by the line you take in your last I fear it would not have given me much satisfaction." There was to be no compromise here:

The fact is our viewpoints are so divergent that the only comfort you could give me would be to withdraw *The Black Girl* and make a public act of reparation for the dishonour done in it to Almighty God. In spite of the book I still have such faith in your greatness of mind that I think you capable of such a noble act and I ask you to do what I should not dream of proposing to a smaller mind—suppress the book and retract its blasphemies. . . . I have made myself responsible in some sense for that soul of yours and I hate to see you treating it so lightly. You do not realise how deeply you have outraged the feelings of those who like myself believe in God and in our Lord's divinity. . . . Let me implore you to do this one thing and withdraw the book.

Shaw's reply was equally uncompromising:

You are the most unreasonable woman I ever knew. You want me to go out and collect 100,000 sold copies of The Black Girl which have all been read and the mischief, if any, done; and then you want me to announce publicly that my idea of God Almighty is the anti-vegetarian deity who, after trying to exterminate the human race by drowning it, was coaxed out of finishing the job by a gorgeous smell of roast meat. . . . You think you are a better Catholic than I; but my view of the Bible is the view of the Fathers of the Church; and yours is that of a Belfast Protestant to whom the Bible is a fetish and religion entirely irrational. You think you believe that God did not know what he was about when he made me and inspired me to write The Black Girl. . . .

Having brought "inspiration" into his rejoinder, Shaw makes a good deal of it, citing God who instructed him when in Knysna to "Take your pen and write what I shall put into your silly head" and then chiding Laurentia for not being pleased with what God had told him to write. Finally he declares that it had been God who insisted that the book be published. The letter ends in a more conciliatory fashion, with Shaw asking that she continue to pray for him; but there is some distancing in that "Brother Bernard" is replaced, as in the previous note, by "G. Bernard Shaw."[29]

What is one to make of this question of "inspiration"? Shaw used the word in his afterword; he repeated it in his dedication of the printed copy sent to Dame Laurentia ("An Inspiration / which came in response to the prayers of the nuns / of Stanbrook Abbey . . ."); and here again he resorts to it as his absolute line of defense. One may remark in passing that his claim in the dedication of the copy sent to Dean Inge—that he did not know whether the "inspiration" came from "above or below" and his frequently repeated assertion that the text was "blasphemous" present a different image of the unrepentant author.

The question of "inspiration" invites one to backtrack to possibly the first letter Shaw wrote Dame Laurentia.[30] It is in the context of her response to *Saint Joan,* and it is with Joan and the nature of her "inspiration" that Shaw deals first. "It was therefore necessary," he tells her, "for me to present Joan's visions in such a way as to make them completely independent of the iconography attached to her religion. But I did not therefore deprive the visions of their miraculous character." Moreover, "The divine inspiration takes the path of least resistance; and whether you believe that the messengers are real persons or illusions . . . the inspiration loses none of its divinity either way."

As with Joan and the "divine inspiration" with which he invests her, so too is his belief in the "divine inspiration" that guided him as an author: "I exhausted rationalism when I got to the end of my second novel at the age of 24, and I should have come to a dead stop if I had not proceeded to purely mystical assumptions. I thus perhaps destroyed my brain; but inspiration filled up the void; and I got on better than ever."

There is no *Black Girl* in contention here, no need to be placating, conciliatory, defensive. This is Shaw declaring his stance as a creative writer. What he produces is the result of "inspiration," and it is "divine." In the same letter, he announces that he wants his sound to go out to all lands, for he has a holy mission to accomplish; anything less than "inspiration" would deprive his mission of the essential constituent of divine truth.

One moves on to *The Black Girl* and the "inspiration" that informs it, no matter that he was aware of its "blasphemous" nature. Skeptics will continue to be skeptical and see the assertion as Shaw's way of trying to preempt the kind of criticism that Laurentia leveled at the book. Mystics on the other hand—and Shaw must be included among them—will see it as evidence of a divine guiding hand beyond mortal control, urging him (paradoxically) to commit his manifest "blasphemies."

Dame Laurentia remained unforgiving. Wedded body and soul to her faith, she could not have reacted otherwise. Shaw had done dishonor to almighty God in her eyes, and given that he was not prepared to withdraw *The Black Girl* from circulation and publicly recant his "sin," nothing short of his banishment from her life could appease her. It was a fierce repudiation, made more so—one suspects—by her failure to acknowledge personal disappointment, for she had made it her mission to bring "the poor wanderer" to salvation in the church. Here now this selfsame wanderer was asserting his right to wield his authorial knobkerry in the most sacred of places. Refined and exalted personality that she was, her set of religious beliefs and, perhaps, a lack of imaginative amplitude made it impossible for her to accommodate this iconoclastic Shaw in her heart and soul.

The relationship broke down: the visits and letters stopped. This, happily, would not be for long. A misunderstanding brought them together again in 1934, when Shaw misinterpreted an announcement of her Golden Jubilee, which she had sent him on the advice of the presiding archbishop. Shaw thought the card announced her death and wrote immediately to the "Ladies of Stanbrook Abbey" to offer his condolences: "[Sister Laurentia] has, I am sure, forgiven me now; but I wish she could tell me so. In the outside world from which you have escaped it is necessary to shock people violently to make them think seriously about religion; and my ways were too rough. But that was how I was inspired."[31]

She had forgiven him, and he, in this letter, was more contrite than he had allowed himself to be in previous correspondence. The friendship continued, surviving one or two stormy passages, until Shaw's death in 1950. Dame Laurentia died in 1953.

Meanwhile, before Laurentia and Shaw had settled their dispute, other less formidable though more wordy opponents had joined in the controversy. These were the writers of booklets and pamphlets who sought to rebut (or to amplify and defend) *The Black Girl*. They add a further dimension to the story.

Rejoinder

The Black Girl invited argument and controversy. Shaw expected it to, believing (as he told the Ladies of Stanbrook) that it was necessary to shock people violently if one wanted them to think seriously about religion; also anticipating that this particular shock would provoke widespread reaction. It did. *The Black Girl* went out into the world, soon—like *Candide*—to become a best-seller, soon also—like *Candide*—to provoke protest, anger, and outrage across the spectrum of Christian orthodoxies

The old lady who publicly burned the book was merely giving vent in her medieval way to a fairly widespread reaction: in denying the sanctity of the Word of the Bible and in treating Jesus and the cross irreverently, Shaw had offended deeply felt beliefs. There was little institutional religion could do about it, apart from shrugging a collective shoulder and relying on the Rock of Ages to withstand the attack, but—and here one may visualize Mabel Shaw and Father Vassall-Phillips hovering like ghosts over developments, rubbing their hands in gleeful anticipation of Shaw's discomfiture—individual rejoinders in the form of pamphlets, tracts, and booklets were a possibility, a modest way of asserting the truth about God and his Savior. By such means would the faithful be protected against the deep damnation of Shaw and his gospel.

This is what happened in the wake of *The Black Girl*. From 1933 to 1935, and thereafter sporadically until the late 1990s, rejoinders of one kind and another were published—one or two repudiating him, one or two "developing" his message, one mocking him. Yet all—the critical and the eulogistic alike—affirmed the continuing impact of Shaw's tale on religious sensibilities. These publications, buried and forgotten though they may have been for over half a century, add their quota to the story and should be revived.

The first of these was Charles Herbert Maxwell's *Adventures of the White Girl in Her Search for God*, which was published in March 1933. A reprint and a second edition (a third impression) followed in the same month. The tract seems to have enjoyed an extraordinary if short-lived success, and the publishers—seeking to make the most of the White Girl's instant fame—shepherded a congregation of Anglican clerics onto the page opposite the title page of the second edition, where their chorus of praise would, one imagines, have resounded among the faithful. The archbishop of York headed the list with a noncommittal, "I have read [*The White Girl*] with great appreciation, and hope to have some opportunity of recommending it." The bishop of Ripon thought it "A charming 'retort courteous' to Mr Bernard Shaw in his own manner. Even he (being an Irishman) will enjoy the rapier play." Among the smaller fry, Canon Guy Rogers drew an analogy that makes one wonder about clerical perceptions of wit: "Charles Herbert Maxwell's reply to Bernard Shaw is brilliant. He has put on Saul's armour and it fits him like a glove. For wit alone [*The White Girl*] is worth reading, and for sincerity and feeling I have seen no reply to touch it." Archdeacon Vernon F. Storr thought the story "thrilling"; the Reverend C. A. Arlington, headmaster of Eton and dean-elect of Durham, said he had read the *White Girl* with "pleasure"; the Reverend F. C. Spurr said it was "fine." Even the *Times Literary Supplement*, reviewing the book on 4 May 1933, allowed that the White Girl "scores some effective hits with her niblick." (The White Girl wields her "niblick"—a no.4 golfing iron—in the manner of the Black Girl and her knobkerry, tapping her guide, a paradoxical Irish dramatist, on his person whenever he utters a "heresy.")

Primed by such commendations, readers may well turn to the text in expectation of scintillating rapier play and thrills, and for a page or two they may not be altogether disappointed. There is even a hint of the clean-cut prose style of the original and some slight flair for paradox:

> "Where is God?" said the White Girl to the dramatist who had so often and so wittily instructed her.
>
> "I will show him to you," he replied, "and you will see that he is not there yet."
>
> The dramatist was a paradoxical Irishman whose red beard had turned white since he had married the black girl. . . . He was fond of digging in the philosopher's garden, but still fonder of standing on

his head in public—the attitude so happily delineated by Mr Beer-bohm. When asked why he did this, he would reply that the position was really correct, and that all other people were mistaken in the position they adopted. He would also point out that many people were willing to pay money to come and see him stand on his head, people who would not have done so if he had been content with an upright position.[1]

Our dramatist likes to make money, one sees. Once, standing on his head, he had demonstrated how kind and just the people were who condemned Joan to death. He made a good deal of money out of that. Later, adopting his favorite position on an apple cart, he had explained that while social-ism was true and royalism false, a king would make a better socialist ruler than an avowed socialist. He made a lot more money for saying that. Then, still on his head, he had told of things that were too true to be good, which people did not find amusing, so this display turned into a "frost," with the dramatist failing to make much money.

The White Girl asks him whether he doesn't find standing on his head uncomfortable. "What else am I to do if I am not to starve?" said the dramatist. "I am so popular when I do it that it provides an excellent means of livelihood. . . . People idolize me as the Paradoxical Dramatist. . . . But I will not accept coppers and tickeys, like the Conjuror. They must pay fifteen shillings or a guinea for a stall, and half a guinea or twelve and sixpence for the dress circle. They pay their money and laugh at my jokes, but very few of them take my good advice or listen to my drastic truths. They go on being wicked and foolish and cruel, and it makes me feel very superior. But they do pay me quite a lot of money" (8–9).

Where this leaves the dramatist is hard to say: is he a promoter of "drastic truths" or a squalid money-grubber? As paradox, it falls flat on its face, and Maxwell does not rise above this.

The White Girl and her dramatist guide then follow the Black Girl's route through the forest, fortunately in greatly abbreviated form, en-countering God No. 1, a bloodthirsty fellow, the dramatist says, who turns out to be sweet and benign and sorrowful. In the tableau that fol-lows as illustration of God No. 1's benignity, he saves Isaac as Abraham is about to stick a knife into him, thoughtfully providing a sacrificial ram in the boy's place. That our dramatist abhorred this kind of sacrifice does not seem to have entered the White Girl's mind, although God No. 1 hurriedly explains that the sacrifice of animals will be expunged from religious worship in time because, as he says, "I love kindness, and . . . the most acceptable offering is a life of obedience, and faith and love" (11).

God No. 2 comes next. He, the dramatist promises, will want to engage the White Girl in interminable argument. There is none of this, because in addition to looking remarkably like No. 1, he is as sorrowful as his predecessor and equally kind and benign. Here this is worked into the story of Job, whose suffering is somehow transformed into the moral that people will have to "learn to be kinder to those who suffer, and braver when they suffer themselves" (13)

Although there is none of the promised argument from No. 2, our dramatist, who has somehow become a stand-up (an upside-down?) Irish comic, tries repeatedly to intervene. He receives several admonitory "taps" on his person by the niblick-wielding White Girl. "Lemme talk, will you. I don't want to be quiet. I want to argue and explain. I'm a nailer at explaining, I am" (12).

They meet Aldous Huxley carrying a Brave New World covered with a lot of crawling repulsive clockwork figures. Then follows H. G. Wells carrying a number of new worlds from which a curious ticking noise emerges. The dramatist tells the White Girl that Sir James Barrie, when living next door to Wells in Adelphi Terrace, could distinctly hear him changing his mind when he produced another new world—hence the ticking noises (16).

Another author, unnamed, appears. He represents the New Morality, which represents the "new freedom" from the "slave mentality" that bound people to the family unit. One is reminded of the public and critical reaction to Getting Married and Misalliance years before, and here now one has a vignette of people rushing through the divorce court leaving confused children in their wake. The White Girl decides in her supercilious way that the New Morality is very like the old immorality (17).

The dramatist takes a short cut through the forest (who can blame him?) and leads his companion to the "conjuror." The homily that the conjuror—who denies being a conjuror—delivers silences the dramatist until the question of love comes up. "God is love; and love gives and gives and goes on giving," the conjuror says.

The dramatist denies this vehemently. Love, he says, only takes. A woman's love is that of a lioness who eats up her mate. "It is a terrible tyranny. Can you imagine heaven with love in it?" (21).

This prompts the obvious answer from the conjuror. The White Girl has found God but feels herself unfit to follow him. She and her guide continue to the edge of the forest, where they observe the Crucifixion in the distance. The dramatist will have none of that. "[D]on't waste time looking at that vulgarity," he says. "Plenty of other people have been nailed to crosses like that" (23). But the White Girl sees her redemption in the scene and announces that from now on her life will be really worth living. Her quest ends here, and her guide makes off into the forest, though whether he does this upside-down or on his feet is not clear.

The excerpts given above reflect scant understanding of Shaw and his beliefs. Maxwell's White Girl is no more than a conveyance for received doctrine, for all her 1930–ish way with the niblick. Lackluster and conformist, she is likely to end her days teaching Sunday school and coaching golf at Anglican summer camps.

The next work is *Bromo Bombastes* by Lawrence Durrell. Aged twenty-one and already a published poet of semi-juvenilia, Durrell was still a very minor figure in the world of letters. *The Alexandria Quartet* was a long way in his future.

Bromo Bombastes—"Bombastic Bromides" or "Platitudes" (more colloquially, "Big Mouth")—is dated 1933, but one may fancifully try to be more precise about this by seeing the playlet (masque?) as a *pièce d'occasion* knocked off for the entertainment of guests during a country house–party during the summer of that year. It is a weird item, only like itself and so different from its companions that discussion of the piece should be presented in parentheses.

It is a squib written in jingling verse, a take-off of Shaw and *The Black Girl* and also obliquely of the T. S. Eliot of "Ash Wednesday" and *Murder in the Cathedral* in their incantatory moments. It is also possibly (in performance) a mock salute to Edith Sitwell, whose *Facade*, famously intoned through a megaphone by the poet to the music of William Walton, enjoyed a vogue in the 1920s and 1930s. Only one hundred copies of *Bromo Bombastes* were printed. As the title page indicates, here given in full (though not in the Gothic print of the original), these were printed for the "enjoyment of the author's friends":

BROMO BOMBASTES

A fragment from a laconic drama

by
Gaffer Peeslake
which same being a brief extract from
his Compendium of Lisson devices

here printed for the delectation and subtile
enjoyment of the author's friends

London
The Caduceus Press 16 Greville Street W.C.1
MCMXXXIII

What this title page also tells one is borne out by the five-and-a-half pages of the text, that, facetious and frivolous as it palpably is, *Bromo* is as near to being a drawing-room undergraduate lark as makes no difference. The cast is:

THE BLACK GIRL   -   -   -   hereafter designated
S.B.G. or Silly Black Girl
A REPORTER   -   -   -   with notebook
BROMO   -   -   -   the necromancer
MILTIADES, SABLE AND CHORUS OF EUNUCHS
A KEEN EAST WIND
Throughout the piece the curtain does not rise

The entire piece is a duologue between the Reporter and the S.B.G., with Miltiades, Sable, and the Eunuchs providing a couple of choral interludes (interjections rather) on the lines of a T. S. Eliot chorus. The East Wind disguised in a beard blows across the stage now and again. Bromo, the "necromancer," is not heard and does not make an appearance, Durrell's ineffably silly point presumably being that this is the point. The scene opens with the reporter and the S.B.G. "discovered" in the boudoir of the latter. He is interviewing her.

SILLY BLACK GIRL: I have been far.
REPORTER: You have been far?

> S.B.G.: I have been far O far away
> On a fruitless quest of many a day.
> REP.: You have been far?
> S.B.G. I have been far.
> REP.: You have been far?
> S.B.G.: I have been far.
> REP.: You have been far away.
> > [*Here a pause during which he makes symbols on*
> > *A roseleaf in goat's blood.*]

So it begins, and so it continues. Plainly the lines have to be intoned, given a singsong lilt; otherwise the jingles would collapse on themselves. "What did you seek?" the Reporter asks, and, after a good deal of to-ing and fro-ing on the question of "seek," he has a reply:

> S.B.G.: Strange as it seems I was seeking God,
> Treading the paths his feet have trod.
> Strange as it seems I was seeking God.
> REP.: God?
> S.B.G.: Yes, God.
> REP.: God?
> S.B.G.: Yes, God.
> REP.: O *God*?
> S.B.G.: Yes, *God.*
> REP.: Gawd.

The Reporter asks what the S.B.G. found. "Not so much as a demi-god," she says. "Only a couple of sheep in pod, / An Arab sheik and country clod / Who looked nothing like God to me." "What a pity," says the Reporter. "An awful shame," responds the S.B.G., and off they go, this time on the theme of "pity," "shame," and "blame," until the S.B.G. says, "It's a Catholic bluff / Hiding a simple fact," which leads to the discovery that they both *love* "facts," which leads at last to the entry of Miltiades, Sable, and the chorus of Eunuchs, who intone a dithyramb on the topic:

> As a matter of fact
> We all like facts
> Better far better than second acts,
> Better much better than Statesmen's pacts,
> And even more than religious tracts.
> It's facts that attracts us

facts that attracts us
facts, facts, facts.
Let's have no subterfuge,
Let's have a deluge,
A cataract of facts.

At this point the East Wind crosses the stage diagonally, disguised in a beard. "What is the fact that you have found?" the Reporter wants to know once this apparition has melted into the wings. At the risk of being indiscreet, the S.B.G. tells him that God is not the man in the street. "Not the man in the street? . . . Not God?" "Not God," she insists. "Gawd," says the Reporter (as though this has not been expected for some five or so exchanges). The East Wind returns, presumably now blowing west to east, and the reader moves on to the next segment in which the S.B.G. agrees to disclose her views for news—under protest, however, because she likes to be pressed. "You like to be pressed?" / "I *love* to be pressed." / "You *love* to be pressed?" / "But under protest"—which launches Miltiades, Sable, and the others into their second dithyramb:

She likes to protest
The sweet coquette.
She loves to protest
And yet . . . and yet
Don't for a second dare to forget
That she's under protest.

"That she's wearing a vest," Sable repeats in an aside, which causes the East Wind to strike her dead with a blow from its beard. Printer's ink gushes out and runs all over the stage. Still pressed for her views for news, the S.B.G. agrees to surrender these to the Reporter. The climax, the revelation, is upon us:

REP.: Your views for news?
S.B.G.: My views for news.
    [*Here a pause during which the EAST WIND crosses the stage*
                    With ink dripping from its beard.]
S.B.G.: Alas, I see I cannot choose
But let you have my views for news.
My story is, though long, in short,
That God resides in Whitehall Court.
REP.: In Whitehall Court?
S.B.G.: In Whitehall Court

REP.: What, Whitehall Court?

S.B.G.: Yes, Whitehall Court.

REP.: Not Whitehall Court?

S.B.G.: Yes, Whitehall Court.

REP.: But . . . God?

S.B.G.: Yes, God.

REP.: What . . . God?

S.B.G.: Yes, God.

REP.: Not . . . *God?*

S.B.G.: Yes, God.

REP.: GAWD.

> [*Here a pause. The East Wind enters and strikes
> an unbelievable attitude. The curtain goes up.*]

One hopes the audience enjoyed this "clever" little frolic. The players—all those bright young things—probably did. As one of the reactions to the Sage of Whitehall Court and his Black Girl, *Bromo Bombastes* should be presented in parentheses.

Dr. W. R. Matthews's (1881–1973) *The Adventures of Gabriel in His Search for Mr Shaw,* a "modest companion," as the subtitle says, "for Mr Shaw's *Black Girl,*" appeared in August 1933. Matthews was no mean adversary. Dean of Exeter when he wrote the *Adventures of Gabriel,* he had made a name for himself as a philosopher-theologian. Later, succeeding Shaw's friend Inge as dean of St Paul's, he was to become one of the most respected churchmen of his day.[2] One of his talents appears to have been a sense of humor, which he did not attempt to hide.

Celestial beings, he assures the reader in his "Prologue in Heaven," are similarly blessed; so it comes as no surprise to discover Saint Peter asking the Archangel Gabriel to go down to Earth to investigate the strange noise coming from a man named Shaw. "Which is . . . the real noise?" Peter wants to know, or, as Gabriel puts it, "Which is the real Shaw?"[3] Arriving on Earth, he disguises himself as a private investigator and sets out in search of Shaw, discovering eventually the "Shavian wilderness," a "terrain without plan and without tracks," and a "strange confusion of sights and sounds" (14–5).

Gabriel hesitates. How is he to discover the real Shaw in this howling desert? But he enters and in due course discovers five different Shaws, the first four illusory, the fifth the real one.

Shaw No. 1 is banging away on a big drum. Why such a din? Gabriel wants to know. To draw attention to himself, says Shaw No. 1: "It's no use having great ideas unless you can get them heard." But isn't the noise inimical to "thinking things out" and "coherence of ideas"? Questioned in this pointed way, Shaw No. 1 becomes abusive. "[Y]ou will be talking about 'absolute truth' soon! Go away and become a modern man." Irritated, Gabriel breaks the drum, and Shaw No. 1 vanishes. "No drum, no Shaw," he concludes. "That means that the Shaw I saw was unreal" (18–22).

Shaw No. 2 is nearby sitting on a rustic bench, an arm round a pretty young woman, lecturing her about love. It is, he insists in a loud hectoring voice, the "Life Force . . . making use of us for its own ends"—a better thing, he assures Gabriel, than the "old stuff about eternal devotion." Gabriel, being an angel, is reticent about offering an opinion but points out that the young woman is fast asleep. Shaw No. 2 leaps up in vexation and fades from view. This is another illusion, confirmed by the young woman who wakes and says, "I dreamt that a perfect lamb of an old gentleman was making love to me. But, goodness, how the old dear did prose" (23–9).

One moves on to Shaw No. 3, the enemy of the learned professions. He has tied a judge, a bishop, and a doctor to trees as if to sacrifice them and, watched by an audience of men and women (but no children), proceeds to insult his audience and then to berate the bishop for being a "dangerous encumbrance" who with his fellow divines goes about preaching a deity whose proper name is "Nobodaddy." They know that the Bible is a collection of ancient and now unimportant legends yet never say so. And when he, Shaw No. 3, writes a little tract to show that the myths of their creed are not plausible enough to take in an intelligent black girl, they either don't read it or, if they do, keep very quiet about it (34, 37). Saying which, Shaw No. 3 sticks a hatpin into the gaitered shin of the bishop. The doctor comes next. Shaw abuses him as "one of the most pitiable of creatures . . . who is financially interested in disease" (38). He is about to stick a hatpin into the doctor when Gabriel intervenes and then discovers that the three learned gentlemen are waxwork dummies, made by Shaw No. 3 himself, who explains that whenever he made up a character he put at least one human feature into it. "It is a point of honour with me. It is not really difficult. Just a question of mechanics" (43).

The scene fades, Shaw No. 3 with it, and Gabriel is left still searching for the "real" Shaw. Will it be No. 4, who is discovered in a high pulpit preaching from a pile of pale green volumes?[4] No, this is another figment, who preaches the gospel of the Life Force with a good deal of proselytizing fervor. "Sweep away the Bible and the principle of Natural Selection, and you have cleared the ground for the religion of the Life Force. That is what I proclaim to you. That is the good news which I bring" (48). Gabriel engages the preacher in a discussion that ends when Gabriel accuses him of being "nothing but a contradiction in terms" (54). Insulted, No. 4 vanishes.

Still searching, Gabriel enters a miniature world, and here he discovers the "real" Shaw, so small that Gabriel has to use his magnifying glass to see him. This Shaw has a consuming interest in drama, which he sees as a potent instrument of spiritual regeneration. "I have sought a firm foundation on which we can build a life which is noble and secure. . . . I have been filled, too, with a rage which is hard to control against the unreason and injustice of human society. . . . When courage and reason could do much, if not all, to procure a dignified and happy life for the majority of men, I am overwhelmed by indignation and despair at the cruelty and folly of our society. Often I laugh so that I shall not weep" (57–60).

Gabriel remarks that these views coincide to a remarkable extent with his own, but how is it, he asks, that you are so small? Shaw No. 5 replies: "How can I get any bigger . . . while all those other fellows live on me? They consume my substance. There is the fellow who will beat the terrible drum, the one who is always philandering, the one who runs the waxwork show, and, worst of all, the bore who is never happy without his pulpit. They have taken the substance which I ought to have had. They have prevented me from growing" (60).

Mission accomplished, Gabriel returns to heaven. He has found Mr Shaw, he tells Peter, "a difficult man to get to know" and "rather on the small side" (62).

The reviewer in the *Times Literary Supplement* did not think much of the *Adventures of Gabriel*. "The present retort from a distinguished theologian is . . . rather a heavy-footed piece of satire."[5] One may disagree. It is true that the premises on which the plot is based are shaky in that Matthews's critique of the four illusory Shaws fails to allow them their roles in Shaw's plays. This is more than overborne by the way he turns Shaw's *Black Girl* upside down and inside out, time-honored devices that here send a celestial being in search of an author who himself had sent a black girl out on quest during which she encounters a fair number of celestial beings who are themselves, in Shaw's book, illusory. There is entertainment in this, no heaviness of foot; also, the four "unreal" Shaws generate tension and propel Gabriel on his quest at quite a jolly pace. For this, one forgives a lot. But why, one wonders, does Matthews shrink the "real" Shaw down so, when it is obvious those four allegedly blustering bullying predecessors could never have consumed his substance?

Another rejoinder, strictly a variation on Shaw's theme, was in the printing press by now: Mr and Mrs I. I. Kazi's lengthily titled *The Adventures of the Brown Girl (Companion to the Black Girl of Mr Bernard Shaw) in Her Search for God*, which appeared in September 1933.[6] Thereafter, like the others, she faded from view to emerge suddenly and strangely in Lahore in 1950.[7] Mr Kazi's local eminence—he was vice-chancellor of the University of Sind in Hyderabad in the 1950s—rather than the intrinsic merit of the book may have prompted this resuscitation.[8]

In spite of the reference to the Black Girl in the title, there is very little "companioning" in the literal sense, at least not at first. She is mentioned together with Maxwell's White Girl, who is resurrected as a platinum blonde named "Miss West" whom the Brown Girl has put through graduate studies in economics and finance. As for the Black Girl, she "had been a student of divinity in her own way, and the Brown Girl's sincere friend. But she had married an Irishman and given up her studies, and since then the Brown Girl had seen very little of her" (3).

The Brown Girl is a pampered darling, "the only daughter of an eastern potentate of fabulous wealth." She owns a two-seater Rolls-Royce and lives in a "gorgeous flat in Mayfair, wherein she could study, revel and sin" (1–2). But something is missing in her life. "Where is God?" she asks the one-eyed beggar-woman, and she begins to find the answer in "History," a stern hoary-headed fellow who appears to her in a dream. He sends her off on a kind of Cook's tour of religious beliefs of the past, traveling through vistas of history from paganism to various more advanced and comparatively recent forms of theism in both the East and the

West. Civilizations come and go in not very stately procession, and the Brown Girl is slave, concubine, companion, and interlocutor in more or less random sequence, receiving as she flits from age to age and sage to sage crash courses in religious doctrine from, among others, Buddha, a pharaoh, Moses, the Greeks, Jesus, and Mohammed. A grand vision of recent history follows: the USSR is seen as a "phoenix rising from the ashes" and the United States as a "great nation in the far west," which— two definite pluses in the authors' opinion—had stopped "drink whole-sale" and "recognized the rights of individuals to put an end to matrimonial connections if they so desired" (88). Just when this vision is about to disintegrate, the Black Girl appears, and there is a touching reunion: "'Oh, I am so delighted to see you here in this grove!' cried the brown girl, kissing her. 'I was really getting frightened,' and looking at her tenderly she continued: 'Haven't we reason to thank that great dramatist; but for whom we would not have the pleasure of having you amongst us?'" (89).

"But for whom," the Black Girl should have retorted, "we would not have had to suffer all this endless prosing." She refrains, having no doubt learned the wisdom of tact since putting her knobkerry aside and marrying the Irishman. Instead she tells the Brown Girl that the White Girl— the platinum blonde Miss West—has fallen out with "my dramatist Love" because "He told her that she could not find God in the way she thought; while she claimed to have found God inside everybody" (89).

The girls enter a vast amphitheater where a get-together of great minds has been organized for their benefit. For Miss West's benefit as well, as it turns out, for that enterprising young lady, faithfully reflecting Mr and Mrs Kazi's image of that great nation in the Far West, shows up not, it would seem, to find God inside everybody but to promote commercial interests. So one has representatives from each of three segments of the world: the Black Girl representing Africa; the Brown Girl the East; and the White Girl, obviously, the West, and also apparently doubling as a look-alike of the well-known actress of the time (Mae West)—a perplexing compounding of roles. Everyone or practically everyone from the first, second, and third worlds appears for the edification of the three girls. Within a page, Goethe, Tolstoy, Plato, the Arabian philosopher Ghazali, and Bacon have spoken, and within another page Hegel and Spinoza. Then Aristotle . . . Herbert Spencer . . . Karopotkin (Kropotkin)

... Carlyle ... Keats ... Shakespeare (a very gloomy Bard). The list goes on and on, but no red-haired Irishman joins the queue; perhaps Mr and Mrs Kazi sensed that this would be taking things too far, he being "real" as opposed to the "unreal" procession of great minds with which the girls have been favored; or perhaps because he had been instructed by the Black Girl to stay at home and look after the children. Whatever the reason, one misses him and the touch of irreverence he would surely have imparted to these dreary proceedings.

What all the pronouncements amount to in the end is that theism "is the natural inborn belief of humanity." This is the contention of the dust cover blurb. The book is also alleged to prove that from "Noah down to Muhammed every prophet preached Islam in its theistic aspects." Be this as it may, it scarcely makes *The Brown Girl* an effective "companion" to, or development of, Shaw's *Black Girl*. At best a repeated lament from the prophets and philosophers one meets that man persists in holding on to outworn creeds may be seen to echo the theme of the original. As a variation of Shaw, it makes a slight point; as a "rebuttal," no point at all.

Four Men Seek God: A Reply to a Famous Author's Book by C. Payne appeared late in 1934. It was noted in the *Times Literary Supplement* of 14 December 1934; apart from this it does not appear to have attracted attention. A disclaimer opposite the first page of text declares that "the names and characters in this book are entirely fictitious and refer to no living person," which may be true of the four men but is glaringly untrue of the "famous author" whose infamous book sends them out on their quests. References to this book come thick and fast in the opening pages, where our four men are discovered in their club engaging in an exciting and heated debate. Their topic is a famous author's book, which had recently been published: "a nauseous book to many minds, yet some of the same train of thought praised it as high-brow literature." Let these four men speak for themselves:

> "It is against human nature," said Sir George, "and, to my mind, the effects on the young, and even on some of the elders, will be disastrous. Pure Atheism—if you can call Atheism pure! The outcome of a twisted, tortured mind. I suppose it amuses the author to write such books, and, of course, there are thousands of people who believe in them."

"The reading public of to-day go mad over an author who deliberately flouts God. They say he is courageous, and not afraid of public opinion!" put in Bilston. . . .

"I cannot understand what the author is getting at in his reference to the blacks," argued Sir Archibald. "Certainly, my experience of the black races is different from that of many. As you know, I have spent some years amongst all kinds of blacks and yellows, and, if you treat them properly, they naturally become your slaves. . . . I tell you, I think this author must have struck something odd to write a book like that—A Black Girl in her Search for God."

Blayne, the fourth member of the group, wonders whether the Black Girl ever found God. The author, he says, omitted to tell his reader. Bilston has a ready answer: one had to have personal experience of any subject before being able to speak or write about it. It was the same with religion.[9] The famous author and his "nauseous" book having been put in their place, to say nothing of the "blacks" and "yellows" who "naturally become [one's] slaves," the four friends agree to embark on independent quests for God.

Sir George Tomkinson, an eminent scientist, begins his quest with a dream (dreams and visions are a feature of the book) in which he listens to a sermon by a latter-day prophet, a shaggy individual with (so the reader is seriously informed) the mind of a Samson and the appearance of Joshua and a line in public confession that reflects the "famous author's" godless career, particularly in its pro-Bolshevik phase. Samson-Joshua inspires Sir George to pursue his quest without delay. His wife humors him, the Bishop retreats in alarm, but his friend Jack, an eminent Harley Street physician (naturally), lends a sympathetic ear. Sir George tells him that the usual four at the club had debated the last book of the "Great Burnet Shore" and, determined to prove it right or wrong, had made a compact to seek God. Jack warns him that there are many imitation gods and religions (13–4).

So it is the Great Burnet Shore himself who is behind all this. Trust him to upset the religious apple cart in his uncouth way.

Sir George, having been advised by Jack, rapidly disposes of a variety of "imitation gods," among them God in the Virgin and Child as depicted in works of art. (This comes to him in another timely vision, in a railway carriage.) After his wife's sudden death, yet another vision is vouchsafed him, a supernatural odyssey rather, for his ghostly guide takes him whizzing through time and space to view a further series of false gods and religions, not excepting Roman Catholicism, until—in what may be intended as a denunciation of Major Barbara's desertion of the colors—he finds Christ in a humble Salvation Army shelter in the East End of London. All this is too much for George. Death beckons, and he summons his three friends to his bedside so that he may testify to having found God. Quite simple, he says; God revealed himself in a vision, which is no surprise, considering the number that came George's way.

He has disposed of most of the "imitation gods" the author can think of, so the quests of his three surviving friends are accordingly shorter. Sir Archibald, a surgeon—also eminent, of course—muses on the death of his friend George, concluding that it is one of those mysteries that will never be revealed. "To the unbelievers, like the author of that book, it would seem that if God was a God of Love, He would never allow such things to happen" (35–6).

The author of that book is not having an easy time of it, but worse is to come. Sir Archibald, who is a "man of the world," can recognize a prostitute when he sees one, and, being a doctor, he knows everything there is to know about social diseases. Therefore, observing a streetwalker, he gives her a wide berth. "Had he been a disciple of the new moral code, he would have acted differently" (40–1). The Great Burnet Shore is of course a founder of the new moral code, which actually approves of prostitution. Witness his scandalous *Mrs Warren's Profession*. If these outcasts and street girls had had "a mother and home like he had," Sir Archibald muses, "they would never be living the life they were doing. 'Home and good parents are the answer to that author's new morality,' he said aloud" (43).

Coincidence, not visions, guides Sir Archibald in his quest. He rushes to the aid of a victim of a street accident. Wonder of wonders, it is his sainted mother, come to London to visit him. He finds God through her, undertaking a retrospective quest through his early years with her and becoming as a little child again.

This brings the reader to the third friend, the businessman Andrew Bilston—not apparently a "Sir" but definitely eminent. His God turns out to be the deus ex machina, who obligingly responds to Bilston's prayer to be saved from financial ruin by giving him heaps of money. Bilston practices a rigid Presbyterianism, a form of Calvinism that prescribes hard honest work as a godly occupation in that it may ensure acceptance among the Elect. If one makes money in pursuit of this way to salvation, well and good; it is a sign of divine favor. So in Bilston's case, the god-in-a-money-box is solid evidence of God. The text does not invite subtleties of interpretation, but the Bilston episode may be a not-so-subtle swipe at the ethic governing *Major Barbara*, where the money that saves the Salvation Army shelter comes from two bloated capitalists, Bodger and Undershaft, certainly not from God.

The fourth friend, Blayne—not a "Sir" but eminent and an "R.A."—also has visions. He has one of a Christ figure, which sends him out into the countryside where, painting near a ruined abbey, he sees the same figure watching him. The scene changes, and the abbey becomes as it was centuries before. The Catholic ceremony Blayne and this figure observe does not celebrate the true God. Christ weeps, and Blayne sees his redemption in the tears.

The four friends have each found God. All the surviving three need do now is castigate that "famous author" and his book, which they carry out with the same plodding earnestness—not to say witlessness—with which they have followed their quests. Their cogitations (to call them that) mount to a pinnacle of bathos in the concluding remarks, where Bilston betrays his failure to recognize Voltaire in the garden, and Sir Archibald exhibits his flawed reading of Burnet Shore's text.

> "The only good part," reflected Bilston, "was where the woman sought God in a garden. As I read it I hoped that the author would have allowed the seeker to find the true God there."
>
> "But don't forget, Bilston," answered Sir Archibald thoughtfully, "that even in a beautiful garden there are weeds and briars and things to destroy, and so it appears to be in this author's mind, though what could have been a beautiful climax is spoiled by the presence of the Irishman. Could the Black Girl have met the missionary who had taught her to seek God, and related her experiences to him [sic], there would have been a very different ending" (76–8).

As Shaw knew all too well, no preaching and pamphleteering, not even a pellucid tale, could penetrate a closed mind.

Marcus Hyman's *The Adventures of the White Girl in Her Search for Knowledge* followed hard on the heels of *Four Men Seek God*, being published in October 1934 and afforded a short notice in the *Times Literary Supplement* on 17 January 1935. It was, the reviewer wrote, not astutely, one of those books that would not have been written but for Shaw's *Black Girl*. Hyman's heroine, Sylvia Swan, is a student at the London School of Physiognomics. A fellow student, George, attracts her, a "tall young Irishman who flaunted a full red beard and kept very much to himself . . . Sylvia had heard much of his intellectual attainments."[10] One day during a student ramble in Kent, she contrives to walk alone with him and is "captivated by his witty and charming conversation." But to her chagrin, he seems to have no interest in her personally, preferring to embark on a lecture on the role of women in the scheme of things.

Adam ate all the fruit from the Tree of Knowledge, he declares, leaving nothing for Eve. Ever since, women who pretend to thirst after knowledge like men are either foolish or perverse. "What greater horror could the devil himself conceive," George exclaims, "than a blue-stocking, that poor unfortunate creature, neither a man nor a woman, sterilizing the natural feelings within her for intercourse and motherhood, cataloguing facts in her brain, and transforming herself into a living reference book? No woman ever produced anything more original than pleasure and children; and that is as it should be, like it or not. . . . Women seeking Knowledge!" he adds contemptuously. "Pshaw!" (16–7).

Sylvia is outraged. The epitome of what today would be called a male chauvinist pig, this young Irishman is neither witty nor charming, and his "intellectual attainments" scarcely pass muster as a parody of John Tanner, whose play, *Man and Superman*, this "George" had probably not yet written. "Did he think," Sylvia thinks furiously, "that men had a monopoly on brain power in the World, that Women were incapable of acquiring Knowledge? Well, she would show him his mistake" (17). Armed with a heavy stick, she enters the Ashdown Forest in search of Knowledge, leaving George leaning against a haystack and haranguing the circumambient air.

Her ensuing adventures come upon her pell-mell and are by and large illustrations of pandemonium rather than Knowledge. First to appear is the Devil, a gorgeous black gentleman, who tries to seduce her while magically divesting her of most of her clothes. Next is Solomon the Wise, who also tries to seduce her while removing what is left of her clothing. Then it is Mr Grundy, whose myopic eyes pop out on proverbial stalks when he sees her naked, and who is revealed when Sylvia makes him take his clothes off as the redoubtable Mrs Grundy herself.

Next in the queue is a "noble Greek"—Plato—who promises a more positive approach to Knowledge but has time only to quote briefly from *The Republic* (Sylvia echoes him later), warn her against the "hemlock of democracy," and suggest that the ideal state may yet be found in Reality. Next is an eighteenth-century dean—Jonathan Swift—with a predilection for addressing his remarks to an oak tree and calling Sylvia "Stella." He is rather offhand about Knowledge but friendly enough to escort Sylvia to Babel and Bedlam (Hyde Park Corner on a more than usually noisy Sunday), where assorted crusaders and revolutionaries are hawking their religious, economic, and political nostrums at the top of their voices. Violence in the form of fascism erupts, and Sylvia flees back into the forest. Here she meets a young woman in golfing attire and carrying a niblick—Maxwell's White Girl, who condescends to Sylvia in a nauseating way. She has found God, she says, having been led to him by the Apostle Maxwell. "I had a conviction of sin, and felt that the Holy Spirit was pleading with me," she says; and again, "The Holy Spirit was pleading with me." Sylvia, remembering her set-tos with the Devil and Solomon the Wise, is thoroughly alarmed by this and advises the White Girl not to be tempted. "Remember Mary," is her ambiguous parting shot.

Hyman explains in an epilogue why he included this scene in his book. *The White Girl in Her Search of God* had struck him as a spiteful but ineffective attack on Shaw within a weak and maudlin affirmation of the Bible. He thanks Maxwell for providing the opportunity to ridicule him.

The next highlight is a take-off of the League of Nations, which assumes the form of a Gastronomic Conference attended by dogs of all nations. Sylvia will recall the dean's satirical remarks about the republic of dogs and the tendency of the leading dog to grab the largest bone and then create either an oligarchy or a tyranny, both of which will lead to civil broils. This happens here. A longhaired dachshund—an illustration shows him sporting a small black moustache—is prominent with a snarling *"Dachshundsland über Alles!"* and a Japanese dog kills a Pekingese. Snarling and bickering continue until the dean flings a huge meat bone among the delegates and a free-for-all ensues.

Next on Sylvia's agenda is the Theosophical Museum advertised by a big portrait of Annie Besant that falls to the ground when the dogs start fighting. Entering this building accompanied by the dean, she observes row upon row of ghosts and souls of animals preserved in jars of pure alcohol; then, going into the Reincarnation Room, she discovers the Theosophical Trees of famous men and notorious types and sees how their souls, pickled in spirits, transmigrate from one species to another. Thus the *Evolution and the Devolution of a Jew-Baiter* is exhibited as starting with the soul of a louse, then metamorphosing to a crab, to a toad, to a reptile, to a rat, to a skunk, to a mongrel, to a moron, and thence finally to a gabbling Jew-baiter. One such exhibit, of an Irish Dramatist, has an illuminated card attached to it with the legend "As Far as Thought Can Reach." The metamorphoses begin with a cabbage and proceed through an elephant, a satyr, a Hebrew prophet, a Chinese Mandarin, and so on to a creature with four heads and no genitals, then a Brainstorm, then an electric flash, and finally an ovum. "The Life Force" is written on the container of the ovum. All this may be a possibly conscious attempt to echo satirically Gulliver's visit to the Grand Academy of Lagado, where a similarly useless and fruitless pursuit of "Knowledge" failed to produce (for example) sunbeams from cucumbers.

Leaving the building, Sylvia meets a "murderous-looking villain," a representative of twentieth-century man, who sings a lugubrious ballad bemoaning the loss of all that was great and good in days gone by. He, least of all the candidates she has met in her quest, can show her the way to Knowledge.

Fortunately the fountainhead is not far off. Sylvia arrives at a clearing in the forest, where she comes upon a glass hut mounted on a high wooden platform. In it, seated at a desk, is a thin, bearded old gentleman dressed in a nightshirt. He looks extraordinarily like the God in *The Black Girl* who nailed Job in argument, but not quite, for his white hair, bushy eyebrows, remarkably high forehead, long nose, and nostrils that curve sardonically do not express self-satisfied cunning but rather a distinctly "mephistophelian quality." Sylvia tells him that she is seeking Knowledge and asks if he can help her. He responds in a soft Irish brogue (Job's argumentative God did not have a brogue, for sure), and she is reminded of the young Irishman she left talking at the haystack. "Get rid of your clothes, sit in the sun, and read *The Intelligent Woman's Guide to Socialism and Capitalism*," the old gentleman says. "I've done all that," she replies, running up the steps and entering the hut, much to the old gentleman's consternation. Echoing Plato, she tells him that her search for Knowledge must imperatively lead to a "Republic where women are treated as more than mere incubators and vehicles for pleasure; where the rulers are chosen from women as well as men; where women and men share the privileges and bear the responsibilities of citizenship equally; where the women are common to all men and children are the children of every citizen."

The old gentleman tells her that he has spent the best part of his life trying to persuade the English to build such a state, but they are too stupid to do so. In Russia, however, his entire stock of ideas had been adopted, and the people—more ignorant on the whole than the English—were putting them into operation. Sylvia declares that they must go to Russia, but the old gentleman demurs. He has just come back from Russia, he says, and has no wish to go back. Why, she asks, had he not stayed?

"Strictly in confidence," he replies "I feared I might change my mind and denounce my own ideas which now form the basis of the prevailing religion in Russia. Such a denunciation would rightly be treated by Mr Stalin as counter-revolutionary, and as I have a natural antipathy to killing of any kind, I came away before they shot me. Besides Russia is still a very uncomfortable place to live in, and life is unbearable without a town and country residence and a couple of cars at least. But I am starting on a world tour very soon and hope to discover the ideal state yet" (56–7).

Sylvia stays with the old gentleman, basking (still naked) in the sun and listening to him sermonizing. The elusive sought-for "Knowledge" seems to have achieved definition in this pairing, and she seems happy. Here, one might expect, her quest will end. But Hyman, whose own "Sylvia" inspired his book, cannot leave his heroine in the arms of "Knowledge" alone, not when personified in a "sermonizing" geriatric gentleman. So he spins out his tale, introducing by way of contrast to the old gentleman a procession of conspicuously unedifying Eminent Contemporaries: "Herbert" (H. G. Wells), who passes by "Making Outlines"; then "Hotaire Billycock" (Hilaire Belloc), eating onions and scowling at "Herbert"; then "Glib T. Tunnerchest" (G.K. Chesterton), swilling beer; and finally "Professor Fundamentalaski" (Harold Laski), followed by a train of adoring males and females.

One person remains: Sylvia's talkative friend, George, who is standing on his head in the clearing. He responds to her call by turning several somersaults and executing a neck-spring before striding to the hut. Sylvia sees the resemblance between the young fellow and the old gentleman at once. So does the old gentleman, who—knowing that "wild young man rather well"—has no wish to meet him again and wastes no time in clearing out. Sylvia wants to know about the projected world tour, and the old gentleman tells her he intends setting off immediately and urgently advises her to chase the young man and get him to marry her.

Sylvia does this, and after some difficulty à la Ann Whitefield and Tanner, she captures George and marries him. She is then so busy setting up home that she has no time to think about her search for Knowledge and the Ideal State, but one may be sure that her days with the old gentleman instilled something of this in her—some "Knowledge" gleaned from all that sermonizing. "Knowledge" in itself is sterile, however—as "George" had indicated in his castigation of the bluestocking female—and has to be applied to life, has to grow to "Wisdom" and the riches that can accrue from this, even unto the third and fourth generation. Hyman's thinking does not go as far as this; he fails to recognize the distinction between the two, and his book ends in the air without full dialectic closure.

It is also overcrowded and lacks focus. The two representations of Shaw as the young "George" and the "old gentleman" are amusing but inaccurate. Even so, the narrative is entertaining and inventive in a racy, high-spirited way, and it makes its point that those who, like Sylvia, reject the false prophets of the twentieth and earlier centuries and cleave to Shaw will grow to fullness of being. As a tribute to Shaw and *The Black Girl* and as a counter to the pieces that had preceded it, *The White Girl in Her Search for Knowledge* emerges with credit.

This was the last of the immediate reactions to *The Black Girl*, and it, together with its forerunners, prompts the obvious thought that all the authors represented here felt bound to respond to the original by means of tales derived directly from *The Black Girl*. Not by tract or pamphlet, not by discourse aimed at rebutting or developing Shaw through reasoned argument. There may have been reactions of this kind from some pulpits in the 1930s, possibly also in stray religious publications, where the Shavian doctrine would have been refuted, but such—if there were any—have been lost to time. It was the tale that seemed to capture the imagination, and it was through the tale that Shaw's opponents and maybe would-be supporters set about securing an audience. There is no surprise in this. The success of *The Black Girl* would have made emulation obligatory; anything other than a narrative would be doomed to swift oblivion, even among the faithful. There is no need to press the point, but there is also no harm in reminding oneself that the drawing power of the "tale" is as old as Homo sapiens, older than the truism memorably penned by Philip Sidney in his *Defence of Poesie:* "With a tale forsooth [the poet] cometh unto you, with a tale which holdeth children from play, and old men from the chimney corner."

Shaw knew this instinctively and applied it in *The Black Girl.* The others, sensing merit in the method, followed the path he had blazed through the Tsitsikamma Forest at Knysna, transforming the forest to suit their particular needs while sending their protagonists out on their quests to discover God. That their tales were an implicit tribute to the arresting nature of the original does not seem to have occurred to them; that by imitating Shaw they were unwittingly flattering his achievement, even when they intended most not to flatter, seems similarly to have passed them by. Yet they all leaned heavily on him, from Maxwell's "dramatist" through Matthews's five "Shaws" to the Kazis' "Dramatist Love" to Payne's "Burnet Shore" and on to Hyman's "George" and "old gentleman": the Shavian persona is there, a commanding presence in every tale. The same goes for Durrell's contribution; his Silly Black Girl would never have been created had the "God" of Whitehall Court not first brought a Sensible Black Girl to literary life.

That these authors were engaged in what later academics, dedicated to the abstract "science" of literature, would call "transtextualization" is neither here nor there. Perhaps they were lucky not to know this.

The run of rejoinders eased after Hyman's Sylvia had married George, although pieces continued to appear sporadically. The first, *The Adventures of the Black Man in His Search for God* by H. M. Singh, is listed in the relevant Cumulative Book Index as having been published in Lahore in 1937. A fugitive piece, it soon vanished, leaving no trace of its existence in major libraries. After this, C.E.M. Joad came along in 1943 with *The Adventures of the Young Soldier in Search of the Better World,* which seemed to promise a reversion to the old formula.

This was so in a way, but not quite. The book was published in 1943 at a time in the Second World War when an Allied victory was assured, and Britain could look beyond the war to a future good life. Joad was one of the best qualified in the country to discuss this future, at least from the common man or woman's point of view. Popular philosopher, member of the popular BBC radio program, the Brains Trust, Fabian, an ardent Shavian whose book on Shaw would appear in 1949, he was one of the best known left-wing intellectuals of the time. Everything that comprised Joad's personality seemed to promise a book in which his young soldier's quest would be along much the same lines as those Shaw had set up for his Black Girl. This does not happen. His young soldier is a far cry from the Black Girl, most strikingly in that there is no religious theme governing his search. Joad tended to flaunt his atheism until he returned to the fold in later life, and there was no way he would allow his young soldier to dally with what he regarded at the time as the most false of false panaceas. As though to add point to this divergence from Shaw, he does not mention him in his acknowledgments, not even to suggest that his title is a crib from an earlier, more famous work. Emphasis by omission could not be more obvious.

This is not to say that the spirit of Shaw—Fabian rather than metaphysical—does not hover over the text. For instance, Mr Transporthouse (the Labour Party headquarters)—a jolly-looking avuncular fellow with a Yorkshire accent (J. B. Priestley, perhaps)—promotes socialist utopias that could have been culled from Shaw's prefaces and Fabian tracts. He remains the young soldier's favorite postwar visionary throughout his quest, which is not a difficult thing to manage considering the unappetizing alternatives he encounters. There is a brutally dogmatic communist robot and an assortment of religious and other cranks, but the most odious is the Red-tape Worm, whose bureaucratic brave new world includes such attractions as a radio implant in the brain. Mr Heardhux—a disembodied voice with a mouth that hovers in the undergrowth like an unamused Cheshire Cat's—speaks at length about the soul and evolution. The imperative of evolution, he says, is that it has to realize itself by enlarging the consciousness so as to achieve the "true end of man." Mr Heardhux's brand of evolution is not Shavian, although he makes one or two points that echo Shaw: "What I have said is that [civilizations] will collapse unless human beings become wiser and better, wise enough and virtuous enough to use the tremendous powers with which science has endowed them without destroying themselves."[11] John Tanner had been going on in this vein some forty years before; Shaw himself in many public utterances since then, including *The Black Girl.*

The final encounter is with a Philosopher whose resemblance to Joad is as close as the red-haired Irishman's resemblance is to Shaw. It is another crib from *The Black Girl.* This Philosopher philosophizes in an engaging way, consigning all but Mr Transporthouse to oblivion for their excesses, demonstrating the "all or none" fallacy and telling the young soldier that "Faith . . . is what makes some people say they believe what they know is not so" (112). Other musings follow, punctuated by Joad's then famous "It depends on what you mean by," until he finally advises the young soldier to work for a better world materially and spiritually, not simply to wait for it to happen.

The Young Soldier has period interest, and at the time it would have been seen as a worthwhile contribution to the debate on postwar Britain. The reviewer in the *Times Literary Supplement* praised it, but it disappoints in resolutely refusing to acknowledge Shaw.[12] Joad would have been fully aware of this; perhaps he looked the other way because he wanted to avoid the religious bias of the original and wanted to write his own firmly antireligious book, even while modeling it along the lines of *The Black Girl*. There is an implicit tribute in this—to someone he admired enormously—and the obvious derivation echoes the original adequately enough.

The next work to be derived from *The Black Girl* has already been granted a premier position in "Antecedents," where it cheekily and on its own merits comes in as a junior partner to Voltaire and Shaw—Brigid Brophy's 1973 *The Adventures of God in His Search for the Black Girl*. This brings the line of reactions to such a bravura climax that one might almost wish the series had ended here. But *The Black Girl* has continued to fascinate and tease and is seemingly indestructible. She keeps on popping up, sporadically and in different forms, most recently in 1999, in a form already well established by custom—the literary pamphlet—and previous to this in adaptations, "dramatizations," one might say, for stage and radio.

The first of these I will consider is the pamphlet *Further Adventures of the Black Girl in Her Search for God* by Donald Sutherland, in which the Black Girl—now named Emma—has reached middle age; her children are mostly grown up; her husband, the Irishman, continues to work in the garden when not popping into the local "hostelry"; and the old gentleman (Voltaire) has died. Emma, now feeling that she can continue her search for God (as Shaw had hinted she would), steps out into a teeming metropolis where churches, mosques, temples—edifices representing different religious faiths—are readily at hand for quick exploratory visits and discussions with the spokesmen of the faiths pursued and practiced in them. Thus, in short order she is given crash courses in Christianity (represented by a deaconess of the Anglican Church), Islam, Buddhism, and Hinduism, among others. Then a Sikh on a motorcycle nearly knocks her over, pausing to explain his religion to her before rushing off. After this, encounters with a number of "fringe" religions come her way, entirely in the streets of the city, beginning with a quarrel between an Irish Catholic and an Irish Orangeman and continuing with a follower of "the most modern prophet, Bala'u'llah," who extols the virtues of a faith that has, so he affirms, superseded those of Moses, Christ, Mohammed, and all the others. After this an atheist—who prefers to be called a humanist—presents his case. Surprisingly, considering Emma's origin, no advocate of African beliefs comes strolling down the street. But it has been a busy day for her, and she is more than ready to return home, where her husband, still in the garden, has been entirely unworried about her long absence and the children troop in to the evening meal without evincing any interest in her adventures. But she is at peace in herself: "[S]he had reached a satisfactory end to her investigation for the moment anyway."

This is a slight, unpretentious tale. It lacks tension, but its straightforward narrative and moments of rhythmic poise keep a reader going. As a "continuation" of the Black Girl's quest it makes little progress; neither does it make any point within its own terms of reference except to suggest that God resides and may be found in any number of faiths, hence to indicate the virtue of religious toleration. It also suggests that a quest of this nature will probably lead the female protagonist back home to her family—and into the kitchen.

Coming now to the adaptations of *The Black Girl* for the stage, radio, and other media, one has to ask: Why did Shaw opt for narrative instead of a play? One recalls that his first thought when stranded in Knysna was to write a play, and he says as much in the first sentence of his preface. Yet when the Black Girl beckoned, he responded in the form of third-person narration rather than direct enactment through dialogue. A critic, James M. Ware, has suggested that Shaw made his choice because "he was aware that his imagination had not realized his thought through the experience of a convincing character."[13] A "convincing character"? Voltaire and Shaw's discussion of "character" in Brigid Brophy's *Adventures of God* comes to mind, where they agreed that "character" in fiction was an overrated criterion. Whether one accepts this or not, the Black Girl is in a line of Shavian ingenues who grow from comparative innocence to wisdom and self-knowledge in the course of their experiences. She is not as fully realized as, for example, Ellie Dunn in *Heartbreak House* or Barbara in

Major Barbara, least of all Joan before the horrors of realpolitik have blotted and besmirched the tabula rasa of her guilelessness, but she is "convincing" enough as she is, more than adequately realized to have acted out her role in a play had Shaw chosen to put her into one.

There are other more substantial reasons that militate against a play, given the form that Shaw's "inspiration" dictated. The episodic and linear plot, for one thing; the kaleidoscope of scenes; the host of characters; the to and fro of discussion and dispute—these all argue against presentation on a stage. I could go on, but the point is clear enough: structurally and thematically, *The Black Girl* is not suitable for a Shavian play, least of all a full-length one.

Yet it seems to cry out for dramatization. There is scarcely an episode that does not bear the imprint of consummate dramatic skill. Shaw could as much avoid this as he could avoid breathing; dialogue was instinct with him, and it is through dialogue, through direct enactment, that the episodes gather momentum and substance. So, even though Shaw himself may have had excellent reasons for not writing a play, a few others following him, observing the built-in dramatic content, have seen excellent reasons for trying to turn *The Black Girl* into one.

Texts for such adaptations, like their productions, are ephemeral. None appears ever to have been published. Texts for this kind of presentation are superfluous, generally being lifted holus-bolus, or almost so, from the original. Two adaptations for the stage—both important in their way because they are conspicuous in standing solitary and alone in time and place—have survived, not in print but, in one instance, in a critic's account of the production, and in the other, in firsthand memory. I will consider each in turn.

The critic was James M. Ware, mentioned above, and the adaptation he described was by the British novelist and man of letters Christopher Isherwood, whose *Black Girl* was staged by the Minnesota Theater Company at the Mark Taper Forum, Los Angeles, from 20 February to 4 May 1969.

This theater is not quite "in the round," but the playing area provides a surround of about two-thirds, which immediately does away with the distancing created by the proscenium arch and, incidentally, does away as well with the technical problems a director would have to overcome in a conventional presentation. A wall behind the playing area was used for projecting various effects made possible by the wizardry of modern stage mechanics and electronics. As Ware recorded, Micah's snarling maw that threatens to swallow the Black Girl was projected, as was a garden of lights for her to tend at the end of her quest. Recordings of African music were played entr'acte; the set was uncluttered, with a few animal masks, a couple of stones, a denuded tree trunk, and one or two other "African" items being deemed sufficient to suspend disbelief, while the stage changed color "like a chameleon" as an aid to suggesting both the variegated leafy patterns of the forest and the fabulous nature of the plot.

Isherwood departs from Shaw's text in the opening sequences by introducing first a group of blacks playing conga drums, dancing, and "generally frisking about." The image this conjures up of something wild and woolly seems a far cry from the stylized conventions of African dance, and one hopes no distorting effect was created. The Black Girl joins the group, greeting them joyfully while they lightly mock her conversion with pious gestures. Ware sees this as an "idyllic scene" that is disrupted by the entry of a woman missionary singing "Onward Christian Soldiers" with her comrades and bearing a large cross. The blacks (but not the Black Girl) hurriedly put on European clothes over their African outfits. Ware makes the point that the auditorium, endowed by the municipality, was not the place to dramatize the contrast between nakedness and clothing that Shaw had in mind. "The satire of white shamefacedness was blunted, but the black girl's costume was inconspicuous, and she was an unashamed *ingenue*." (One remembers Shaw's comment to Yeats about Farleigh producing a series of woodcuts for an Irish edition of the book in which the Black Girl would be depicted in a skirt; and, as will be seen, the question of nakedness and clothing is central to the Black Girl's rejection of the image maker's "art.")

Referring to the political undertones of Shaw's text, Ware suggests that *The Black Girl* had been chosen for production "less for its theology than for its pertinence with the American obsession with race relations. Shaw could see the invisible black man." It is an important observation, which I will discuss further in the next chapter. That *The Black Girl* raised racial-political issues in America in the 1960s and continues to do so worldwide today goes without saying.

As for the text and the production, Isherwood or his director—probably doing the best he could with a small company—used a "quick-change artist" to play several parts from Jehovah to the Irish gardener, all of whom were identified in the program as "Shaw." Generally Isherwood adhered to the text, inserting snippets from the preface, and even though, as Ware says, the world premiere of the play did not cause a splash, *The Black Girl* proved to be stageworthy.

The other adaptation of *The Black Girl*, as retrieved from memory and communicated to me by coproducer Susan Hussey, was staged by the Gorilla Theater in Tampa, Florida, on 9, 10, 16, and 17 March 1991. The other producer was her husband, Aubrey Hampton, who also directed. The venue was the Hillsborough Community College in Ybor City, a predominantly black section of Tampa, Florida. The production was sponsored by "Saturday's Children," an enrichment program for children of color.

This production, like Isherwood's, departed from the text in its initial "stage-setting" preamble, with a local rapper performing a rap he had specially composed for the occasion. He wore fatigues and sunglasses and carried a boom box, with which he would no doubt have put his audience into a receptive (and amused) frame of mind. The adaptation itself appears to have adhered to Shaw's text fairly closely, which is not to say that the staging did not take certain inventive liberties, bringing out the comedy in several amusing ways. One scene, the Black Girl's confrontation with the Caravan of the Curious, was presented as a tea party. (A tea party in darkest Africa—how very colonial and British, and risibly appropriate!) The actress, Lori Bassett, who played the Black Girl and wielded a knobkerry artistically fashioned by a local black woodcarver, dominated the stage with her beauty and moral conviction, her sheer star quality. Susan Hussey comments, "We felt ourselves very lucky to have found her."

The production went down well, playing to near-capacity houses in a 300–seat auditorium. Audiences were predominantly black. It is in this context that Susan Hussey echoes James Ware's remark about race relations in America: "The production was especially meaningful to me because I discovered how much racism simmers under the surface of our community—it is so invisible to us whites living in our white parts of town. I visited parts of town I had never gone to before . . . and it made quite an impression on me. Thanks to the genius of Shaw for making this possible!"

There have apparently been no repeat performance of either Isherswood's or Hampton's versions; nor have other adaptations that would qualify as live theater surfaced.[14] Television similarly draws a blank, and although the Society of Authors has had enquiries about possible feature films, nothing has come of these. (*The Black Girl* could be effective as animated cartoon film, but this is highly unlikely to be made. Disney and his kind would reject it, given the costs involved and the certainty of box office failure and denunciation in the far-flung and vocal world of religious fundamentalism.)

Stage readings, either solo or with a cast, are another matter, though not spectacularly so. Apart from a few isolated performances of this kind (by Louis P. Solomon for the Chicago Shaw Society on 21 May 1957; and at Wisconsin State University on 1 May 1967), Dan H. Laurence's adaptation has been occasionally presented by Laurence himself at the New York Public Library (22 September 1961) or by a full cast, possibly with some doubling of roles, as at the Shaw Festival at Niagara-on-the-Lake on 16 July 1999.[15]

A notable stage reading was presented at the Mermaid Theatre in London on 22 February 1967, when Basil Ashmore produced an adaptation, together with Shaw's short story "Aerial Football," with Edith Evans and John Westbrook in the cast.

Radio is another story, and in the 1930s, the British Broadcasting Corporation—enjoying an absolute monopoly of the airwaves in Britain—was the obvious body for possible adaptation of the tale.[16] Shaw's association with the BBC was well established by the 1930s. A member, then second chairman, of the Advisory Committee on Spoken English, he was also the corporation's favorite playwright and oversaw (from his homes in Whitehall Court and Ayot St. Lawrence, both before and after performances) the production of many of his plays from the early years to his death in 1950. These productions, some thirty in all, included, in 1924, *O'Flaherty V.C.*, the first of his plays to be broadcast and read by Shaw himself, *Saint Joan* in two parts, *Captain Brassbound's Conversion*, *Arms and the Man*, and others. Each of these provides a story in itself with staff members of the BBC drama division treading warily round the "Great Man," as they referred to him, while he, increasingly cantankerous and critical of their efforts, peppered them with irate "corrective" postcards.

The saga of *The Black Girl* began on 13 June 1940, when a staff member, the scriptwriter Hugh Stewart, sent an in-house memorandum to a certain "DR": "If we can get Shaw's permission, I am anxious to make an adaptation of [*The Black Girl*]. Would a radio version of it be all right from your point of view?" A jotting below this, presumably by DR to a certain "GD," states: "Any comment? It is a year since I read it—have you a copy?—& I thought it showed a colossal ignorance of Biblical Crit. since 1880." DR's response—he is now "DRB"—to Hugh Stewart is dated 17 June 1940: "We certainly have no objection to your broadcasting an adaptation of the story if you can get Shaw's permission. I think, personally, that the excellent story is based upon a totally inadequate knowledge of what Biblical scholars have been doing during the past fifty years, and that it is founded on an antiquated attitude to the Bible—but that gives us no right to turn it down. So go ahead! It would be rather fun if we could follow the broadcast by a discussion in which the pundits could attack Shaw's position." One thanks the powers that be that this notion of "fun" fell by the wayside before *The Black Girl* was broadcast.

Hugh Stewart went ahead and wrote to M. T. Candler of Programmes Copyright on 18 October 1940: "I believe there was no commitment on our part to show Mr Shaw the script of the radio adaptation of [*The Black Girl*]. Would you let me know about this point? I do not want him to see it unless absolutely necessary." Programmes Copyright responded on 25 October: "I told Shaw when negotiating with him about 'The Black Girl' that if he wanted to see a copy we should be pleased to send him one. He did not however say anything in reply. So I do not think there is any need to let him see it." The BBC seems to have gotten away with this, and *The Black Girl* had its premiere on radio on the Home Service on 3 March 1941. Shaw does not appear to have raised an objection, and later, on 26 April 1941, Candler made bold to mention to Shaw that the broadcast had met with "quite a remarkable response." However, when another BBC director, B. H. Alexander, approached Shaw on 22 May 1941, two months after the premiere, to repeat the broadcast at the same rate of thirty guineas, he got a capitalized "NO" for an answer. "Ask Val Gielgud why" (24 May 1941). Val Gielgud was the director of BBC drama. Ensuing correspondence does not spell out the reason for Shaw's refusal, but it is possible to infer that it was the quality of the readings rather than the adaptation (Stewart's work) that had displeased Shaw. Alexander, prompted by Gielgud, wrote to Shaw on 26 May 1941 to ask whether he would be willing to allow the BBC to broadcast their adaptation if a suitable colored actress could be found for the part. Shaw replied, but quite what he said is not clear, as this letter, like others in the BBC files, is missing.[17] but it is again possible to infer that the casting had not satisfied him, because

Alexander next wrote to ask whether it would be agreeable if Elizabeth Welch took the part. Shaw agreed, and *The Black Girl* was presented in a new production on 19 June 1944, three years after the first broadcast, on the Home Service in the BBC Starred Programmes. This was repeated on 5 January 1947 on the Third Programme.

These performances ended BBC radio adaptations of *The Black Girl* in Shaw's lifetime. Since then, according to the records held by the Society of Authors, the Australian Broadcasting Corporation in Sydney broadcast an adaptation on its National Service on 25 January 1951; the BBC repeated its 1947 production in August 1953; and a BBC production in Urdu was broadcast in two parts in Pakistan on 13 and 20 December 1964 (testimony to the interest aroused by *The Black Girl* in the East). To conclude this list, Dan H. Laurence's version—recorded in a reading performance at Niagara-on-the-Lake Shaw Festival in 1999—was broadcast by the Canadian Broadcasting Corporation Radio 1 in its Sunday Night Playhouse on 27 February 2000 and repeated in Monday Night Playhouse the next evening.

This, for the time being, concludes the reactions, the responses, and the adaptations, but there is no telling when and where and in what guise Shaw's Black Girl will reappear.

Champion

The story of *The Black Girl*—the episodes comprising her quest—may be allowed to answer for itself. It is simple, suspenseful in its own charming way, tightly constructed, seamlessly developed. It is probably the best, certainly the most read, narrative Shaw wrote, and it remains in print and in demand, Penguin Books having last reissued *The Black Girl and Some Lesser Tales* in 1999.

Important though it is, the story is no more than the sugar round the pill, the inducement to get readers to swallow it all, the sugar and the hard core of thought within. This was Shaw's style. A "triple thinker," he would load his texts with subtexts by which as apparently simple and artless a tale as *The Black Girl* would convey layers of themes and ideas, gathering density of texture as it proceeded. To refer to John Farleigh's illustration, now on the title page, the tale is like the tendrils and creepers of the Black Girl's forest, twining and twisting round and in and out of one another, rich in ferny undergrowth, hiding green thoughts in green shade.

Three such "layers" should be isolated from their contiguous growths: the religious, the feminist, and the political (or racial), within each of which the Black Girl will emerge as a "champion," becoming a twentieth-century Athena, issuing from the head of her creator and uttering her war cry as she pursues these causes.

I begin with the religious theme, because, as the title and preface indicate, Shaw's primary concern—the initial impulse—in his tale was the state of religion "at the present world crisis."[1] As such, it debunks not the Bible itself—which Shaw regards as a superb work of literary art and "much more alive than this morning's paper and last night's parliamentary debate" (preface, 10)—but the unquestioning veneration that has accreted round it, leaving everything in it inviolate and inviolable from the beginning and on through the centuries. In Shaw's words, "that lazy and sluttish practice of not throwing out the dirty water when we get in the clean" has resulted in stagnation where a crystalline fountainhead of vital religious belief should exist (preface, 13). As he also remarks, "It is the Bible-educated human who is now the ignoramus" (preface, 12).

The Black Girl, though "Bible-educated," refuses to be an ignoramus; she is determined to find God for herself. In this and in setting out to discover God, she hints at qualities she will soon exhibit more fully: strength of mind and spirit that will enable her to withstand and reject not only the false gods of the past as represented in the Bible but also the false gods of the present as represented by science, by Islam, by art—by all the falsehood and error lurking in the forest. In this she is like a medieval knight questing for the Holy Grail or like Bunyan's pilgrim, incorruptible and resolute in resisting and overcoming the powers that attempt to entrap and subdue her. In this she emerges as a "champion" of the modern soul's search for divine verities.

Then she encounters an old gentleman—Voltaire—tending his garden; later she meets the Irishman—Shaw—working in the kitchen garden. These two encounters constitute the summation of her quest, the resolution of the religious allegory, and the Black Girl's acceptance (for the time being) of the two faiths presented to her. They should be considered, though it has to be said that Shaw's text, for all its limpidity, is so densely textured that no more than a generalized appraisal is feasible.

Voltaire, having invited the Black Girl into the garden (by which he allows her to establish her claim to its riches), soon expounds his Deistic theology:

> Make a little garden for yourself: dig and plant and weed and prune; and be content if he jogs your elbow when you are gardening unskilfully, and blesses you when you are gardening well.... [W]e shall never be able to bear His full presence until we have fulfilled all His purposes and become gods ourselves. But as His purposes are infinite, and we are most briefly finite, we shall never, thank God, be able to catch up with His purposes. So much the better for us. If our work were done we should be of no further use: that would be the end of us; for He would hardly keep us alive for the pleasure of looking at us, ugly and ephemeral insects as we are. Therefore come

in and help to cultivate this garden to His glory. The rest you had
better leave to Him. (68)

The old gentleman has prefaced this with a cautionary tale about Semele
and Jupiter, the moral being that an infinite and perfect God is eternally
beyond human capacity to realize, let alone endure. Hence his advice to
the Black Girl to abandon her search and settle for gardening as token of
recognition of His glory.

The delicacy of phrasing in Voltaire's speeches—the poetry in the
prose—is more than sufficient indication of Shaw's veneration of the old
gentleman, and of his respect for the old gentleman's beliefs. Voltairean
eighteenth-century Deism, as outlined here by Shaw, is plainly the forerunner of his twentieth-century Creative Evolution in many respects.

He could not give Voltaire wholehearted support, however. He had
himself, as he declared to Dame Laurentia McLachlan, abandoned rationalism fairly early in his career and adopted the stance of the mystic, or,
as he would say, the guidance of "inspiration." Rationalism brought one
to a dead-end, as he would have seen it, and was essentially static. A static
God meant that humankind was also static; and Shaw, born post-Lamarck
and growing up amid the intellectual and religious revolution brought
about by the theory of evolution (no matter how much he inveighed
against the "Infidel Half Century" brought about by neo-Darwinism),
rejected Voltairean statism, refusing absolutely to accept such a condition
in a plainly imperfect universe.

So the red-haired Irishman comes into Voltaire's garden, which is a
"very amateurish" affair, plainly in need of updating and upgrading, of
being brought out of the eighteenth century into the twentieth. As the
Irishman tells the Black Girl: "That oul' fella is cracked and past his work
and needs somewan to dig his podatoes for him. There's a lot been found
out about podatoes since he learnt to dig them" (68–9). He is soon ex-
pounding his faith:

> "Then you did not come in to search for God?" said the black girl.
> "Divvle a search" said the Irishman. "Sure God can search for me
> if he wants me. My own belief is that he's not all that he sets up to
> be. He's not properly made and finished yet. There's somethin in us
> that's dhrivin at him, and somethin out of us that's dhrivin at him:
> that's certain; and the only other thing that's certain is that the

somethin makes plenty of mistakes in thryin to get there. We've got to find out its way for it as best we can, you and I; for there's a hell of a lot of other people thinkin of nothin but their own bellies." And he spat on his hands and went on digging.

. . . But nothing would ever persuade him that God was anything more solid and satisfactory than an eternal but as yet unfulfilled purpose, or that it could ever be fulfilled if the fulfilment were not made reasonably easy and hopeful by Socialism. (69)

The difference between Voltairean Deism and Shavian Creative Evolution is obvious. Equally obvious is the social message in the Irishman's declaration, which is that those hell of a lot of people thinking only of their bellies have to be fed (on an improved quality of "podato," as it were) before they can strive for spiritual succor. Meanwhile the Irishman and the Black Girl have to find out, by trial and error, how best to "dhrive at him"—how best to achieve the point where a Semele (or an Athena-like Black Girl), so far from cracking like a flea in Jupiter's fire, can look God in the face as an equal and, like Major Barbara, declare him to be in her debt. There is scarcely any need for the Irishman to say as he does that he is a socialist and that the basic principle of socialism, a fair deal—a square meal—for all, is a basic tenet of this faith. And there is no need for the narrator to point out (which he does not) that this garden, representing the world in all its diversity and richness and emblematic in both *Candide* and *The Black Girl* of God's munificence, will henceforth be cultivated in obedience to the decrees of socialism.

This, in broad terms, is the religious allegory underscoring the Black Girl's adventures. Shaw has given the religious question greater depth than this, however, in setting his tale in Africa, in (as he saw it) a fallow continent, religiously speaking, where its peoples—conceivably the progenitors of the next, a black, civilization—should ideally develop their own religious faith. One recalls his remarks to this effect in his first interview on his arrival in Cape Town and his old Fabian ally Sydney Olivier's comment on the same theme. Olivier spoke feelingly about the "fundamentalist formulas" Christian missionaries in the West Indies felt bound to inculcate in their converts. Shaw had no need of firsthand experience to ponder the same issue; he went further than this in depicting the missionary who inadvertently sends the Black Girl on her quest as having improvised doctrinal responses and invented evidence on the spur of the moment in trying to answer the Black Girl's "unexpected interrogative reactions" to her teaching.

As Shaw relates, "the life of Christ, as she narrated it, had accreted so many circumstantial details and such a body of home-made doctrine that the Evangelists would have been amazed and confounded if they had been alive to hear it all put forward on their authority" (22). In other words, the missionaries were inculcating fundamentalist formulas with the added bonus of fabricated doctrine and spontaneous myth-making. What bothered Shaw was the effect of such teaching on Africans, for, as he saw the situation, the consequence would be to graft falsehood presented as divine truth on young souls before their potential for a healthy apperception of the truly divine had had a chance to be realized. This, to him, was an effrontery that could not be brooked—the spiritual rape of innocence, no matter if performed with the best of intentions. As he said in his first Cape Town interview (12 January 1932): "The best thing would be to develop their intelligence and make them sceptics." To make them, that is to say, like his spiritual "champion" of Africa—a Shavianized Black Girl.

Those fundamentalist formulas and ready-made myths built into the biblical tales do not apply only to zealots in the mission field. They abide in a wide range of contemporary Christian faiths, in spite of the unruffled reaction by the majority of reviewers and critics in 1932. To most of them Shaw's religious message was "old hat," the repetition of what he had been saying for years. However, the Roman Catholic reaction was far from being so forgiving. One recalls the Irish Censorship Board, which banned the book; Dame Laurentia McLachlan, who damned the book; the critic-reviewer for the *Catholic World*, who said Shaw was moving to madness. If this was the reaction of a church of the far right, that of the far left would have been no different, cleaving to a literal reading of the Word of God as revealed in His Holy Book—cleaving as well, particularly among revivalist crusades, to "the conjuror" rather than to Jesus. Ironically, then, the Catholic world and its anti-Catholic counterpart would have been at one in this respect, and at one in denouncing *The Black Girl*.

Whether the situation has changed—whether those with a Shavian cast of mind still see that the book has work to do in the world—is hard to say. There has been a considerable relaxing of Catholic attitudes, due to a series of ameliorating encyclicals, particularly Vatican II, over the past forty years, but one hesitates before the door of "Protestant" fundamentalism as maintained throughout the Christian world. Here the religious message of *The Black Girl* would still be regarded as blasphemous, "relevant" only in that it enunciates the Word of Satan, whose wickedness must eternally be driven from the soul of man, born as he is in sin. Shaw's "corrective" theology may, then, find itself more easily accommodated in contemporary views of the Bible but not everywhere; and his "new" theology of Creative Evolution not anywhere. Apart from resistance to this on religious grounds, there is the intervention of science; and this brings the discussion to another issue—the role of science in the modern world and Shaw's attitude to it in *The Black Girl*.

Science is the new theology: its decrees seem to govern everything today; and it has debunked the Shavian belief in the "will" as a genetic property passed down from one generation to the next, thus producing an ever-evolving, ever-improving species. Such entities as "soul," "spirit," and "will" have no place here because they cannot be scientifically verified; yet here, as Shaw insisted throughout his life, the most outrageous sin of neo-Darwinism and of the "new science" in general was to banish soul from the universe, banishing with it the will proceeding from one generation to the next to grow to something greater than oneself. This will to grow, in the Shavian canon, could not be denied, and it is (significantly) the naturalist in the Caravan of the Curious who emphasizes the point, specifically about inheritance: "If you believe in evolution . . . you must believe that all habits are both acquired and inherited" (51–2). Moreover, as the Black Girl tells Ecclesiastes the Preacher, "Life is greater than death, and hope than despair. I will do the work that comes to me only if I know that it is good work; and to know that, I must know the past and the future, and must know God" (30). If such a vision, transcending time and incorporating as it does a knowledge of Good and Evil, of God Himself and the Will to reach Him—if such immortal longings still need to be propagated, and perhaps they should, *The Black Girl* is there to affirm them, let the "new science" say what it may.

Yet not all science was damnable in Shaw's eyes. Even one or two members of the Caravan of the Curious have passing moments of insight, and in his first interview after landing in Cape Town, Shaw spoke of the "tremendous moral force" that science was beginning to exert in the world. He touches on the same theme in his preface to *The Black Girl*: "At present one party is keeping the Bible in the clouds in the name of religion, and another is trying to get rid of it altogether in the name of Science. Both names are so recklessly taken in vain that a Bishop of Birmingham once warned his flock that the scientific party is drawing nearer to Christ than the church congregations. I, who am a sort of unofficial Bishop of Everywhere, have repeatedly warned the scientists that the Quakers are fundamentally far more scientific than the official biologists" (preface, 7).

"Drawing nearer to Christ"? Yes, in the sense that those new "podatoes" the Irishman cultivates in his garden represent scientifically improved agricultural practices, hence more food for the starving multitudes of the Earth, while Shaw's advice to South African agriculture, given during his address in the Cape Town city hall, to draw essential mineral nutrients from the air (has the world got there yet?) is similarly "moral"—scientifically, socialistically so. (One may recall again the naturalist in the Caravan of the Curious who gives it as his opinion that their mistake had been not to offer the Black Girl some food [55].) Any scientific advance that improves the lot of suffering mankind, and not only in agriculture, is "nearer to Christ." This may be typified as the enduring science of nature. It is the genuine article, the Voltairean and Shavian ideal, and it is this—not the damnable heresies of the infidel half-century—that draws the Black Girl into the garden.

Shaw is the unsung feminist of the twentieth century—unsung because he was the wrong gender. The irony that the prototypical champion of women's rights should be ignored (Shavian feminists excepted) has its cause deep in the female psyche, for only a female, the rubric runs, can be a true-blue feminist. It is a doctrine of exclusivity maintained by the belief that only a female can begin to know and understand what it is to be female. Males are, well . . . males, therefore quite incapable of identifying themselves with the physiology, the psychology, the essence of womanhood. Moreover, they are the natural enemy by definition, the ones who have repressed and suppressed women throughout history, denying them legal status, political status, economic status, sexual status, intellectual status, professional status—in a word, all the prerogatives and privileges that should by rights be accorded an individual, irrespective of gender, in any society, democratic or otherwise. There is understandably some warrant for the excesses of militant feminism over the past century, and now, the cause being won, it has perhaps begun to temper its stridency somewhat. Even so, it would do the feminist movement no harm if it permitted the thought—unpalatable though it may be—that some rare male souls, for all their shortcomings as males, entered into the battle on their side and made considerable contributions to their struggle. Shaw was preeminently one of these.

There is no need to detail his crusades on behalf of women. His personal convictions about women's rights, enforced throughout by socialist doctrine, run through his nondramatic writings like a refrain, through his activities as a public man, through his speeches in campaigns that range across the spectrum of life, from public toilets to women's suffrage. They are a constant of his plays, where his gallery of female characters constitutes one of the splendors of modern dramaturgy: his heroines possess a force of personality and an independence of mind that often relegate their male counterparts to subordinate roles. Feminism could have no more inspiring ideal than that embodied in, for example, Ann, Barbara, Jennifer, Lesbia, Hypatia, Lina, Eliza, Joan.

And the Black Girl. The fact that Shaw's protagonist is female has already been touched on, his model the young black women who lived round and about Knysna, her gender determined by artistic and biological necessity. A female then, alone in a wilderness of males and one or two sexless females: the natural flag-bearer of Shavian feminism.

She comes across as an attractive (though rather formidable) personality, very much in the tradition of the Shavian women named above, which is to say inflexible and resolute in asserting her right of self-determination. Add to this her occasional pertness, her refusal to be browbeaten by males, her predilection for asking difficult questions, her readiness to take up her knobkerry to enforce her point of view—add these qualities and one has the first African suffragette. She remains true to her feminist cause throughout; and—this is new—she is naked throughout.

This, her nakedness, Farleigh's illustrations of which seem to have aroused the libido of so many male reviewers and readers, is an aspect of her feminism. The critic Ware commented on this in his review of Isherwood's stage adaptation of the tale, where the clothing worn by other characters was seen to denote the hiding of something obscurely shameful, while the Black Girl's nakedness reflected absence of shame, reflected instead a glorying in her womanhood. She is, spiritually speaking, an innocent, an empty vessel seeking divine sustenance; she is also an Eve who refuses to fall: original incorruptible Woman.

As such, she is more than capable of confronting her male adversaries, notably the image maker and the Arab. The first exchange focuses on this question of nakedness, plus the denial of female divinity in the artifacts the image maker produces (60–1). She points to an image of Pan, who is half a god and half a man, and declares that it is very true to nature, for she herself, she says, is half a goat and half a woman (that is to say, a female aware of her sexuality), though, she adds, she would like to be a goddess (a female transcending her sexuality). But why are these gods never half a woman? So the image maker points to his statuette of Venus, and she promptly asks why the lower half is hidden in a sack. "[S]he is ashamed of half her body, and the other half is what the white people call a lady," she declares. "[T]o my mind she has no conscience; and that makes her inhuman without making her godlike."

Why "no conscience"? Because here Venus, the goddess of love, rejects her specifically female sexuality, which is a rejection of nature. Instead, ashamed of her female attributes, she is inhuman in her denial of the god within her, debasing it by her false modesty, therefore without a conscience. By contrast, the Black Girl's nakedness represents the affirmation of all aspects of the love the statuette hides in a "sack."

The conjuror, resting comfortably on his cross, has an answer of sorts, though he tends to sidestep her point: "The Word shall be made flesh, not marble. . . . You must not complain because these gods have the bodies of men. If they did not put on humanity for you, how could you, who are human, enter into any kind of communion with them? To make a link between Godhood and Manhood, some god must become man."

This is Christian doctrine, the conjuror speaking for his genuine self, Christ, while also anticipating Voltaire's cautionary tale about Jupiter and Semele; but the Black Girl is ready with her feminist rejoinder, a telling inversion of the conjuror's argument: "Or some woman become God. . . . That would be far better, because the god who condescends to be human degrades himself; but the woman who becomes God exalts herself."

It is appropriate here to consider the Black Girl's mistaken transliteration of "the division of the square root of minus x is the key to the universe," as proclaimed by a spectacled lady in the Caravan of the Curious. The Black Girl hears this as "Mynah's sex" and asks where this "root" may be found, being told that it "grows in the mind" and is "a number" (49, 52). She reverts to "Mynah" a short while later, telling the image maker, who denies the existence of such a goddess, that "She most surely exists . . . for the white missy spoke of her with reverence, and said that the key to the universe was the root of her womanhood and that it was bodiless like number, which has neither end nor beginning. . . . Only the truth of number is eternal. . . . Therefore I feel that there is something godlike about numbers" (62).[2]

The Black Girl's preoccupation with "Mynah"—who does surely exist as the immutable and absolute abstraction of number—ties in with what she says to the image maker about a woman who, becoming a god, exalts herself, and who, aspiring to achieve the eternal, will have in her hand the "key to existence." She confutes the conjuror in asserting that the Word would be made number, not flesh, and is here, in her untutored yet intuitive way, reaching out beyond "sex" to a state of bodilessness in infinity.

An Arab (Mohammed) who is present reenters the debate. He has already invited the Black Girl to become one of his wives, promising her much "happiness," to which the Black Girl, asserting her independence of spirit (and Shavian scorn of mere "happiness"), responds that it is not "happiness" she seeks but God. Now the Arab asks Allah to be his refuge from all "troublesome women," the Black Girl being the most troublesome he has ever met. She becomes even more "troublesome" as the discussion proceeds to take in the question of marriage, specifically that practice of polygamy accepted by the Islamic faith (64–5). "A man needs many wives and a large household to prevent this cramping of his mind," the Arab declares. "He should distribute his affection. . . . Until he has known many women he cannot know the value of any." Thus, intriguingly, Shaw eschews the question of middle-class Christian "morality" to give the issue an abstract economic basis, as though the shade of W. S. Jevons—the prophet of Fabian economic policy—is hovering over the exchanges. The Black Girl responds in kind by asking whether the Arab's wives are also to know many men in order that they may learn their "value." "I take refuge with Allah against this black daughter of Satan," the Arab cries vehemently, obviously getting the worse of the argument. He tells her to hold her peace when men are talking and wisdom is their topic, evading the fact staring him in the face that the Black Girl is wise beyond her years, more wise in her feminine (and feminist) way than the Arab or the image maker can be. By way of a self-congratulatory clincher he asserts, "God made Man before he made Woman."

The Black Girl has a ready answer: "Second thoughts are best. If it is as you say, God must have created Woman because He found Man insufficient." And she now adds to the question of value the question of "right" by asking by what right the Arab demands fifty wives while condemning them to one husband. "[H]ow is she to know your value unless she has known fifty men to compare with you?"

It is on this conflation of "value" and "right," skillfully worked into the argument, that the Black Girl rests her feminist case, for of course the woman has equal, perhaps greater, "value" than her male counterpart, and every "right" the male arrogates to himself should be allowed the female. Driven into a corner but refusing to admit to defeat, the Arab can do no more than call Allah to his defense, which amounts to the admission that it is Allah who is unjust: "[I]t plainly appears that injustice to women is one of the mysteries of Allah, against whom it is vain to rebel. Allah is great and glorious; and in him alone is there majesty and might; but his justice is beyond our understanding." This amounts to the admission that Allah's injustice is just. It is a retreat into denial and contradiction.

The feminist argument wins comprehensively, but of course no male will acknowledge this. "I shall not find God where men are talking about women," the Black Girl says as she leaves, and it is the image maker who shouts after her, "Nor where women are talking about men." Are these irreconcilable differences? Not quite, for if the male can acknowledge the equal "value" of women and accordingly afford them commensurate "rights," the differences could vanish. The Black Girl has struck a forceful blow for feminism.

This does not end her campaign. She will marry the Irishman and in due course—to echo Shaw's words to Mabel Shaw—naturally and unaffectedly fill her lap with babies. This, in Shaw's view, was as nature decreed, as the Black Girl herself accepts when observing, "we cannot go against nature" (71). It is in this condition as wife and mother that she achieves contemplative peace, even seeing how funny it was that an unsettled girl should start off to pay God a visit (53–5). Shaw's—the Black Girl's—feminist campaign ends here.

In the eyes of contemporary militant feminism this would be an ending in defeat, for a conclusion that sees the heroine settling into the "slavery" of domesticity with a husband and children amounts to a denial of everything the cause stands for. This may be so. God—the feminist God—may and can be discovered in any number of self-fulfilling ways, the only proviso being the right to exercise life choices not dictated by traditional gender "imperatives." On the other hand, it may not be so. The point is that the Black Girl does exercise her right of choice and abides by it, finding herself as near to God in her adopted role as Shavian theology can bring her. A feminist champion in her own right, she is also the potential mother of the superman, after all.

Shaw's feminist argument seems to falter in what seems like a failure to recognize that the Black Girl comes from a polygamous society and could be the daughter of a first or a second or a third wife (the number depending on her father's status and wealth). As a rebel against her father's harsh treatment of her, including his attempt to sell her to a white "baas-soldier," she has broken free of tribal custom; then as a convert to the missionary's version of Christianity, she would have been taught that such African tribal marriages were "immoral"—although as a skeptical (Shavian) convert she may well have taken the view that this was a typically *bourgeois* attitude. It is not an important issue, and possibly Shaw dismissed it as irrelevant to his central argument, being uninterested in the "morality" or "immorality" of monogamy or polygamy (or the polyandry the Black Girl cheekily introduces into her argument with the Arab). His principal interest was the status and rights—the justice—allowed, or not allowed, women within marriage systems.

The Black Girl in her other role, as the champion of "Black Power," should now be considered; that is to say the Black Girl as a racial-political icon.

"The whirligig of time will soon bring my audiences to my own point of view. . . . " This is Shaw toward the end of his preface to *Three Plays for Puritans*. The whirligig of time is never more rapid than in politics, where whim, fashion, causes, campaigns, crusades, and ideologies can turn the "correct" into the "incorrect" seemingly overnight. Of all the ideologies and genocidal policies thrust into the history of the past seventy years, none has been more perennial and pervasive and terrifying than that of race, linked as it usually is with the doctrine of the racial (or ethnic) superiority of one group over another. It was the bedrock of European colonial policy regarding the Negroid peoples of Africa for over a hundred years. It was established by custom and law in the white settled regions of southern Africa for over three hundred years. In South Africa in 1932, Shaw saw it all about him; he saw through it all, and his Black Girl gave vent to his outrage in damning terms.

Anyone who roundly and loudly condemned racial discrimination, embedded as it was in the immutable law of custom, would have to be an exceptional individual. One remembers Shaw's remarks—repeated in the book—about the next civilization being a black one; one remembers as well the central tenet of his socialist faith that all people were equal, which he found abused to the utmost in Cape Town and Knysna. The Black Girl and her people were the dispossessed of the land; denied the vote, property, everything, they were held in subservience by the iron law of white power. The blacks were the great UN-equal, and his heroine had to be the living contradiction of the doctrine that upheld it—a manifestly superior individual. Shaw made her this, a "champion" endowed with heroic qualities: moral courage, physical and mental strength, good looks, quick-wittedness, a healthy reserve of skepticism, and tons of common sense—a born leader. Who else but such an exemplary female could denounce the prevailing evil and dare to look to a future where blacks have regained their freedom? She will come to do this when, during her quest, she faces the white men and women who comprise the Caravan of the Curious (46–55). The lady ethnologist of the expedition prompts her outburst with a comment about the white man being "played out" and "committing suicide as fast as he can."

> "Why are you surprised at a little thing like that?" said the black girl. "Why cannot you white people grow up and be serious as we blacks do? I thought glass beads marvellous when I saw them for the first time; but I soon got used to them. You cry marvellous every time one of you says something silly. The most wonderful things you have are your guns. It must be easier to find God than to find out how to make guns. But you do not care for God: you care for nothing but guns. You use your guns to make slaves of us. Then, because you are too lazy to shoot, you put the guns in our hands and teach us to shoot for you. You will soon teach us to make the guns because you are too lazy to make them yourselves. You have found out how to make drinks that make men forget God, and put their consciences to sleep and make murder seem a delight. You sell these drinks to us and teach us how to make them. And all the time you steal the land from us and starve us and make us hate you as we hate the snakes. What will be the end of that? You will kill one another so fast that those who are left will be too few to resist when our warriors fill themselves with your magic drink and kill you with your

own guns. And then our warriors will kill one another as you do, unless they are prevented by God. Oh that I knew where to find Him! Will none of you help me in my search? Do none of you care?"

Shaw had been saying this on different occasions throughout his South African visit; he had been saying it for years. He is saying it again here, within his fiction. It is scarcely a case of unwarranted authorial intrusion: *The Black Girl* is an allegory, and didacticism is its web and woof. However—and this is a standard feature of Shaw's didactic-dramatic method—his artistry has submerged his own voice and given the passage telling dramatic immediacy in the Black Girl's voice, suffused her lines with passionate intensity, made her artlessness the vehicle of such compact forceful rhetoric that manner and matter cannot be separated from one another. One notes the swiftly flowing sequence of outbursts—delivered in thrusting staccatolike phrasing—that impels the argument forward, one indictment piling on the other and turning an apparently uncomplicated text into densely textured prophecy. The doom-laden warning is conveyed in the word "gun," repeated throughout, providing a thudding ground bass, like African drums, as though portending endless terror where brute power rules and God has been abandoned. The godlessness of white colonial rule will spread the gospel of godlessness among its subject peoples until murder itself will seem a delight. This is the horror that history will unfold. Set against it, the Black Girl's concluding cry from the heart is the reminder that only God can overcome such evil—the God to whom she beseeches the godless ones to direct her.

Turning on a "huffy gentleman" who argues that the white man's guns have saved the blacks from the man-eating lion and the trampling elephant, she responds with the unassailable argument that such beasts are natural enemies and ask for no more than their due in nature. "They spared our souls," the Black Girl cries. "When they had enough they asked for no more. But nothing will satisfy the white man's greed: You work generations of us to death until you have each of you more than a hundred of us could eat or spend; and yet you go on forcing us to work harder and harder and longer and longer for less and less food and clothing."

The rapacity and inhumanity of white exploitation spares no soul; it grinds the subject people into the dust; its proponents serve false gods and are heathens and savages, knowing neither how to live nor to let others live. "When I find God I shall have the strength of mind to destroy you and teach my people not to destroy themselves."

This was written in 1932 in the heyday of colonialism, when Britain, Portugal, France, Belgium, and South Africa "possessed" Africa; it was written a full quarter-century and more before a black man, still less a black woman, would dare voice such thoughts in public. The Black Girl, the embodiment of the future, was well ahead of her time (as Shaw was ahead of his). As for the other prophecies built into this devastating outline of European colonial policy in Africa, Shaw was right here as well. He was one of the first whites, perhaps the first, to declare "Africa for the Africans," and a half-century ahead of Europe in foreseeing the winds of change that would tear colonial rule to shreds. "The whirligig of time will soon bring my audiences to my own point of view." The whirligig did. The world has now accepted the view, not always willingly, that colonialism—based as it was on the policy of racial discrimination, racial superiority, and the right to exploit subject peoples—is a disgraced episode of history.

The same goes for the policy of apartheid as applied in South Africa until the early 1990s, officially since 1948, semi-officially since 1652 when the first white men settled at the Cape, bringing of course their guns with them. Apartheid was colonialism in extreme form, its roots going deep into the land it had conquered by force of arms and spreading through the body politic like tentacles, its malign effusions corrupting the outlook of black and white alike. What Shaw saw of its workings in 1932 and again in 1935, when he and Charlotte visited Durban, disturbed him profoundly. He avoids specific charges against South Africa in *The Black Girl*, but it is obvious that what he observed firsthand, and what gave force and direction to many of his utterances, informed his thinking when writing the book.

Has postcolonial Africa, now having won its freedom, found God? That was the Black Girl's devout summating wish; she would lead Africa to Him. Shaw may have hoped for something like this once the godlessness of white colonialism had been banished. History has not progressed that far yet. Africa seems at present to have fulfilled only the direful prophecy contained in the Black Girl's words about murder seeming a delight to warriors corrupted by guns and the most devilish intoxicant of all—power. Is this a legacy of colonialism? Some say it is.

Shaw, for all the timelessness of his vision, was caught in time: terms and terminology that occur in *The Black Girl*, considered acceptable in South Africa (and elsewhere) in the 1930s, have been sent spinning by our whirligig into the disuse bin where they now molder, verbal emblems of a rejected past. The power of a word lies in its connotations, and several crop up that are "incorrect" today for precisely this reason: they connote and seem to perpetuate the myth of racial superiority and can be powerful triggers to racial anger. The first is "baas." The Black Girl addresses more than one of the characters by this term. It is of Dutch origin, taken into Afrikaans, and means "master." In the South Africa that Shaw observed, no black, not even a mature adult, would call a white man anything other than "baas," and if the "baas" were a youngster, he was addressed by the diminutive, "basie." The word can be used innocently as denoting "boss," but as used in white-black relations it was the universal verbal token of subjection, of enforced and admitted inferiority and therefore—the whirligig of time doing its bit—to be abolished. (Verbal habits die hard, and still today one hears "baas," but contemporary connotations have blunted the edge to denote recognition of authority—something like "Sir" or "Mister.") One wonders whether Shaw was being ironic when his Black Girl accosts Ecclesiastes the Preacher (among others): "Excuse me, baas. . . . You have knowing eyes. I am in search of God. Can you direct me?" (28) Perhaps there is irony here, and the Black Girl uses the word so as not to seem presumptuous, but it is more likely that Shaw allowed himself to accept common usage of the time.

Another word is "piccaninny," by which Shaw refers to the Black Girl's children. Its precise meaning denotes a small child, specifically a child who is native to the country. The word comes from the Spanish (or possibly Portuguese) as used in the West Indies, but Australia, South Africa, and other countries adopted it and applied it to nonwhite, usually aboriginal children. Racial pigmentation—race—inevitably came into the application, with it the stigma of discrimination and implied inferiority. So the word today is not acceptable, and "child" or "children" is required to take its place.

The third word on this list is in the title itself: "girl." The whirligig of time brings all kinds of pressure to bear on the lexicon, sometimes apparently spontaneously, as in the American use of "disinterested" to mean "uninterested," or "convince" to take over the work of "persuade." Sometimes it is social pressure of the kind that has rendered the traditional meaning of "gay" all but meaningless. (What, today, does one make of Yeats's once glorious lines: "Their eyes mid many wrinkles, their eyes, / Their ancient glittering eyes, are gay"?). Sometimes it is sociopolitical as in "girl." Shaw uses the word correctly as denoting a young female. However, in South Africa and the British colonies, this absolutely innocent word (as Browning used it, "all the little boys and girls with rosy cheeks and flaxen curls") was corrupted to denote an adult African female worker, often a domestic worker. ("My 'girl' is becoming impossible: she now refuses to work on Sundays!") The male equivalent is "boy," as in "garden boy," but Shaw does not use the word, referring with verbal and connotative exactness to the bearers accompanying the Caravan of the Curious as "men." Here, with "girl," the racial implication and its pejorative connotations would be unacceptable.

What about "black"? This seems to be acceptable, although it is often avoided because it implies differentiation, if not discrimination. So at least Shaw's heroine can be granted her pigmentation and continue to serve her people as the champion of a possible future "black civilization."

It is the Irishman himself who uses the most blatantly racist language, when told by the Black Girl that she intends marrying him. "'Is it me marry a black heathen niggerwoman?' he cried piteously, forgetting all his lately acquired refinement of speech." (70) The joke is against the Irishman, certainly not the Black Girl, whose personality and the role she has played transcends the denigration implicit in terms like these. She has rendered their connotations meaningless, as Shaw himself found them meaningless in light of what he observed in South Africa.

One hopes that editors of future printings of *The Black Girl* will not attempt to "sanitize" the text by eliminating these politically incorrect words. They are harmless in themselves in the context of the story and provide not disagreeable period touches.

The racial issue does not end with the Black Girl's confrontation with the Caravan of the Curious. She marries the Irishman, and they produce some charmingly coffee-colored children. In 1935, back in London after having visited Durban, Shaw gave the London *Daily Telegraph* a self-drafted "interview" in which it emerges that his conjoining of the Black Girl with the Irishman was no whimsical afterthought.[3] Here are excerpts from the "interview," which appeared under the headlines

MARRIAGES OF WHITE AND BLACK
Startling Plan by Mr Shaw

Means of Peopling South Africa
"Too Much Sun for Light Skins"

Mr Bernard Shaw has returned home from South Africa an advocate of mixed marriages between the white and black inhabitants.

By this means, he suggests, the white population of South Africa can solve the vital problem on which, in his view, its very existence depends. . . .

He has come back tremendously impressed by the extraordinary pleasantness of the climate. But it is the wonderful sunshine which is creating the danger.

CAN WHITES SURVIVE?

"The question," he said, "is beginning to arise whether white people can survive in these places. I do not mean that you die of the climate—you don't.

"The question is whether your descendants will breed. . . . South Africa does not fill up. It is not a question of birth control, because many people there are desirous to have children but they do not have them.

"I suppose it may be there is too much sunshine for people with white skins. The probable remedy for them is to darken their skins.

"This means, in South Africa, by marrying blacks."

"Would not such an idea be highly repugnant to white people?" I asked.

"Well," replied Mr Shaw, "there are a great many half-breeds. . . .

"In South Africa the mixture of the two colours may provide the solution to the problem. It is not a question of black and white. In the first place there is no such thing as a white man on the face of the earth: the Chinese call us the pinks, very properly.

"The Zulus are a remarkably superior type of person, and all attempts to keep them in an inferior position seem to break down before the fact that they are not inferior. Certainly when you see them working you wish you could see British workmen working that way."

Mr Shaw suggested that the problem was not confined to South Africa, but extended to a very large part of the African continent.

"People," he said, "are speaking glibly now of giving the Germans back their colonies. There is Abyssinia on which Mussolini is thinking of laying his hand.

"You may parcel the country out among the European powers, but at the back of it one day Africa will say, 'None of you will have it.' Africans, whether Afrikander, black, white or anything else, will see that Africa belongs to the Africans and not to so many competing European powers.

"There may be a mixture of blood, and so on, but the native has a good deal of capacity: in the long run it may be seen that he has the capacity to live in Africa and the others have not."

Shaw's starting point in this "interview"—that the climate was causing sterility among the whites—is absurd, and one wonders who or what induced the thought. The population ratio of whites to blacks of about one to six may have caused him to think along these lines, particularly as whites were not producing Victorian-size families any longer and faced a future in which they would be increasingly outnumbered. Whatever the cause, his development of this view—that the interbreeding of whites and blacks in South Africa would improve and unify the races—is not wrong so much as dated. His argument is derived from the theory of eugenics, which—propounded by Galton in the nineteenth century—argued the case of selective breeding to improve human stock. (One may recall his comment, when embarking at the end of his first visit, about "the absolutely degenerate people" he had seen around Knysna, people who were "absolutely hopeless as stock for South Africa," which is pure Galtonese; Tanner in *Man and Superman* was attracted to the idea; Hitler applied it in his breeding and genocidal programs; some nations have tried to implement it by controlling the immigration of "inferior stock.") Eugenics in agriculture and animal husbandry is still practiced, but its application in human procreation is so controversial and uncertain of outcome—to say nothing of the stigma of "social engineering" attached to such a program—as to have been rejected out of hand. Nevertheless, it was taken very seriously in the first half of the twentieth century, and if Shaw sounds like one of the members of the Caravan of the Curious here, implicitly endorsing a "marvelous" fad of the time, one should realize that it is hindsight that informs such a view. And he had already provided his model in the marriage of the Black Girl and the Irishman—a model for South Africa and colonial Africa as a whole, for the future when Africans will have reclaimed their land, and white inhabitants and their descendants, themselves "Africans," would have to find a way of surviving perhaps more than the climate.

When leaving South Africa at the end of his second visit, only weeks before his "interview" in the *Daily Telegraph,* he recommended racial fusion and the abolition of legislative barriers between the races. Put your house in order and quickly, he said in effect, otherwise there would be "a lot of bloodshed and the cutting of throats. . . . I can see you people in a pretty mess before you get everything cleared up."[4] It could be that his comments on the effect of the climate on white fertility were built on this uncompromising scenario; that he was pointing beyond population ratios to what he discerned as an inevitable process of history: the collapse of white hegemony and its policy of racial discrimination, the condign punishment that would fall on the godless ones, the fulfilling of the Black Girl's prophecy. Perhaps this unofficial Bishop of Everywhere was advocating miscegenation, as exemplified in the marriage of the Black Girl and the Irishman, as the solution to racial strife; perhaps it was his way of saying, "Make love, not war—for God's sake."

Notes

Unless otherwise stated, all references to Shaw's work are to the *Standard Edition of the Works of Bernard Shaw* (London: Constable, 1931–50).

Abbreviations Used in the Notes

The Black Girl: The Black Girl in Search of God and Some Lesser Tales (1934; reprint, London: Constable, 1954).
CL1: Bernard Shaw: Collected Letters, 1874–1897, edited by Dan H. Laurence.
CL2: Bernard Shaw: Collected Letters, 1898–1910, edited by Dan H. Laurence.
CL3: Bernard Shaw: Collected Letters, 1911–1925, edited by Dan H. Laurence.
CL4: Bernard Shaw: Collected Letters, 1926–1950, edited by Dan H. Laurence.

Chapter 1. Antecedents: Voltaire and Others

1. The question whether *The Black Girl* is an allegory, a fable, a parable, or even (Michael Holroyd's lighthearted contribution to the issue) a fairy tale is academic rather than real. Shaw referred to it as a "pamphlet," and reviewers seemed to favor "parable" when the book first appeared. I have settled for "allegory," a choice I see no reason to defend. "Knysna" is pronounced "Nigh-zna." It is Khoi (Bushman) for "friendly" or "friend."

2. For a fuller, more discursive account of Shaw's two visits to South Africa in the 1930s, see Hugo, "Upset in a 'Suntrap': Shaw in South Africa."

3. *The Rationalization of Russia*, edited by Harry M. Geduld, was published in 1964 by Indiana University Press. The *Times* (London) published extracts as "Shaw's Theory of Revolution" in April 1964.

4. Preface to *The Black Girl*, 3.

5. I am indebted to Michel W. Pharand for this insight. However, the opinions expressed are my own, not Professor Pharand's. See Pharand, *Bernard Shaw and the French*, 218–20, 256.

6. Ibid., 219.

7. Ibid., 218.

8. Rolland, *Liluli*, 3.

9. Lanson, "Voltaire at *Lés Delices* and at Ferney," 97–8.

10. 20 May 1891, *Music in London*, 1:190.

11. "The Quintessence of Ibsenism," 18–20, 22.

12. 25 October 1891, *CL1*:165.

13. "Epistle Dedicatory to Arthur Bingham Walkley," xxiv–xxxiii.

14. Circa August 1905, *CL2*:552.

15. "Preface for Politicians," 36–7.

16. "Preface: First-Aid to Critics," 221.

17. Preface to *Getting Married*, 202.

18. "Parents and Children," 87.

19. *Great Catherine (Whom Glory Still Adores)*, 154.

20. Ibid., 167–8.

21. Ibid., 181–2.

22. *As Far As Thought Can Reach*, 221.

23. Preface to *Saint Joan*, 24–5.

24. *The Black Girl*, 65.

25. Brophy, *The Adventures of God in His Search for the Black Girl*, 118–9. Hereafter this work will be cited parenthetically in the text.

26. 30 January 1928, *CL4*:8

Chapter 2. Foreshadowing

1. May 1927, *CL4*:53.

2. Laurence's annotation, *CL4*:55.

3. 5 July 1927, *CL4*:56.

4. Undated typescript; *CL4*:56.

5. 16 July 1927, *CL4*:57.

6. 30 January 1928, *CL4*:88–90.

7. *CL4*:88.

8. 17 February 1929, *CL4*:90.

9. 12 May 1930, *CL4*:187.

10. Laurence's annotation, *CL4*:55.

11. *The Black Girl*, 21–2.

12. "G.B.S.," *Cape Argus* (Cape Town), 11 January 1932.

13. 15 January 1932, Holograph, Bernard Shaw Papers, Add Ms 50520, British Library.

14. Shaw, self-drafted interview, *Cape Times* (Cape Town), 12 January 1932.

15. Vassall-Phillips, "G.B.S." This report tends to sensationalize Father Vassall-Phillips's article by highlighting the stridency while omitting references to his deeply felt disturbance of spirit at what he interpreted as Shaw's anti-Christian

utterances. Vassall-Phillips died at sea in May 1932, when on his way back to England from South Africa.

16. Shaw, letter to *Cape Argus* (Cape Town), 23 January 1932.

17. Vassall-Phillips, "Reply to Mr Shaw."

18. As evidence of Shaw's equanimity in the face of malicious criticism, one may point to his reaction to possibly the most vicious attack ever directed at him, with Alfred Noyes its probable instigator, in *Blackwood's Magazine* (Edinburgh), May 1907. Shaw's reaction was to quote a line of verse about young heroes going adventuring.

19. Laurence's annotation, *CL4*:275.

20. 25 January 1932, *CL4*:274.

21. Shaw's address was published as a verbatim report in the *Cape Times*, 8 February 1932.

22. See *The Apple Cart*, act 1, 215–7; *Back to Methuselah, The Thing Happens*, 121 passim; and "Civilization and the Soldier," *Humane Review* (London), January 1901; see also Hugo, *SHAW: The Annual of Bernard Shaw Studies*, edited by Stanley Weintraub and Fred D. Crawford (University Park: Pennsylvania State University Press, 1989).

Chapter 3. Accident

1. Bernard Shaw Papers, Add Ms. 63192, British Library.

2. The ostrich feather was an item of high fashion, particularly in the Edwardian era; Charlotte and Shaw were Edwardians if they were anything, and one remembers the boa (made of ostrich feathers) with which Ann Whitefield tries to ensnare the unresponsive Tanner. See *Man and Superman*, act 1.

3. Shaw, letter to *Cape Times* (Cape Town), 22 February 1932.

4. Patch, *Thirty Years with G.B.S*, 72.

5. 15 February 1932, *CL4*:276.

6. Bernard Shaw Papers, Add. Ms. 56493:1059F, British Library.

7. *CL4*:280–1.

8. *The Black Girl*, 22.

9. Ibid., 46 passim, 55 passim.

10. See *The Adventures of the Black Girl in Her Search for God*, (1932), 11; and *The Black Girl*, 25.

11. *The Black Girl*, 30.

12. Ibid., 32.

13. Ibid, 56. "Tickey" was banished from the South African English vocabulary when a decimal currency was introduced in the 1950s.

14. See Holroyd, *Bernard Shaw*, vol. 3, *The Lure of Fantasy, 1918–1950*, 182.

15. 12 [14] April 1932, *CL4*:280–3. The appellation "Dame" is conferred on Benedictine nuns after they have made solemn profession and served the order for many years.

16. A conflation of reports in the Cape Town newspapers *Cape Times, Cape Argus,* and *Burger,* 18 March 1932 and 25 May 1935.

17. 17 February 1932, *CL4*:277.

18. Hu OHS George [pseud.], "George Bernard Shaw at the Wilderness."

19. Shaw, self-drafted interview, *Cape Argus* (Cape Town), 18 March 1932.

Chapter 4. Publication

1. These quotations and others on this topic are taken from Laurence's annotations to Shaw's letter to Dame Laurentia McLachlan, assigned to 2 May 1932, *CL4*:288–9.

2. *CL4*:289–90.

3. Laurence's annotations, *CL4*:295–6.

4. 8 May 1932, *CL4*:296–7.

5. Unless otherwise stated, all quotations from Farleigh's *Graven Image* in this section are from chapter 8, "The Black Girl."

6. Farleigh, *Graven Image,* acknowledgments, n.p.

7. *CL4*:297.

8. The publishing history of *The Black Girl* is taken from Laurence, *Bernard Shaw: A Bibliography,* 210–2.

Chapter 5. Reaction, Censorship, Repudiation

1. Farleigh, *Graven Image,* 268. Further quotations from this work are from this and the following two pages.

2. London: Constable, 1934.

3. Olsson, "Dressing Mr Shaw's Black Girl."

4. Primary source not located. Probably MacCarthy's review was from the *Sunday Times* (London), for which MacCarthy was writing in the 1930s.

5. See MacCarthy's notices in the *Speaker* (London), 28 November and 2 December 1905.

6. From Wearing, ed., *G. B. Shaw: An Annotated Bibliography of Writings about Him,* vol. 2.

7. "Fable on Religion Published by Shaw," *Times* (London), 6 December 1932.

8. Some slight liberties have been taken with elision marks in this presentation.

9. "Shaw the Prophet," *Times Literary Supplement* (London), 8 December 1932.

10. "Shaw Writes Parable," *New York Times Book Review,* 26 February 1933.

11. "Bishop Attacks Shaw," *New York Times,* 24 December 1932.

12. Shaw to Floryan Sobieniowski, 24 July 1933, *CL4*:347.

13. "Wexford Beekeepers and Mr Shaw: Removal of Membership Proposed," *Times* (London), 30 December 1932.

14. "Wexford Beekeepers and Mr Shaw," *Times* (London), 27 January 1933.

15. Ervine, *Bernard Shaw: His Life, Work, and Friends,* 525.

16. *Sydney Olivier: Letters and Selected Writings,* 14–5.

17. MacKenzie, 28 November and 1 December 1932, *The Diary of Beatrice Webb,* "The Wheel of Life," 292–3.

18. Betten, *The Roman Index of Forbidden Books,* 52–3.

19. Corish, *The Irish Catholic Experience,* 244.

20. *CL4:*339. This information has been gleaned primarily from Laurence's annotations.

21. 4 September 1933, *CL4:*352–3.

22. Wall, "Shaw: The Black Girl Problem."

23. "A Nun of Stanbrook," "The Nun and the Dramatist," 415–58. Most of the account that follows is derived from this source.

24. For a detailed account of the relationship, see Holroyd, *Bernard Shaw,* vol. 3, *The Lure of Fantasy, 1918–1950,* 211–7 and elsewhere.

25. Ibid., quoting Cockerell, 215.

26. *CL4:*281–3.

27. Also in *CL4:*344.

28. *CL4:*344–5.

29. *CL4:*349–50.

30. 23 December 1924, *CL3:*896–8.

31. 3 October 1934, *CL4:*380.

Chapter 6. Rejoinder

1. Maxwell, *Adventures of the White Girl in Her Search for God,* 7. Hereafter this work will be cited parenthetically in the text.

2. See Matthews's obituary in the *Times* (London), 5 December 1973.

3. Matthews, *The Adventures of Gabriel in His Search for Mr Shaw: A Modest Companion for Mr Shaw's Black Girl,* 13. Hereafter this work will be cited parenthetically in the text.

4. The "pale green volumes" are Shaw's *Collected Works,* 1930–32, augmented 1934 and 1938.

5. "Mr Shaw's 'Adventures,'" *Times Literary Supplement* (London), 14 September 1933.

6. As noted in the *Times Literary Supplement* (London), 15 February 1934.

7. Kazi and Kazi, *Adventures of the Brown Girl (Companion to the Black Girl of Mr Bernard Shaw) in Her Search for God.* Quotations from this work are from the 1950 edition, which will be cited parenthetically in the text.

8. Uncorroborated testimony in an unknown hand on the cover of a copy in the Dan H. Laurence Collection, University of Guelph.

9. Payne, *Four Men Seek God: A Reply to a Famous Author's Book,* 3–6. Hereafter this work will be cited parenthetically in the text.

10. Hyman, *The Adventures of the White Girl in Her Search for Knowledge*, 15. Hereafter this work will be cited parenthetically in the text.

11. Joad, *The Adventures of the Young Soldier in Search of the Better World*, 104. Hereafter this work will be cited parenthetically in the text.

12. "In Search of a Better World," *Times Literary Supplement* (London), 4 September 1943.

13. Ware, "Shaw's 'New' Play: 'The Black Girl,'" 11–15.

14. I am indebted to Jeremy Crow, Head of Literary Estates, Society of Authors, for information on performances of *The Black Girl* on stage and radio since 1950 (the year of Shaw's death).

15. Laurence's adaptation has been published by French.

16. "The Bernard Shaw Files," BBC Written Archives Centre, Reading, England.

17. By the 1930s, Shaw's letters and signature had become collectors' items, worth hoarding or selling in the requisite marketplace. One has to ascribe the apparent tendency to remove letters from the BBC files as token of this awareness among members of staff. One or two conscientious souls, presumably overcome by guilt, made typed copies of the originals for the files.

Chapter 7. Champion

1. Shaw, preface to *The Black Girl*, 19. Hereafter citations of Shaw's preface and of the text of *The Black Girl* will be given parenthetically in the text.

2. "Mynah's sex" was in the original 1932 edition; Shaw changed this to "minus one" in the 1934 and subsequent editions; the original has been reinstated for the sake of the pun, though at the cost of strict accuracy regarding Einstein's relativity theory. See *The Portable Bernard Shaw*, edited by Stanley Weintraub, 636.

3. "Marriage of Whites and Blacks," *Daily Telegraph* (London), 11 June 1935.

4. Abstracted from reports in the *Cape Times* and *Burger* (both of Cape Town) and the *Star* (Johannesburg).

Works Cited

The following abbreviations have been used in the bibliography:

Editorial leader	EL
Verbatim report	VR
Partial verbatim report	PVR
Self-drafted interview	SDI
Review	Rev
Report	Rep

Primary Sources by Bernard Shaw

Principal Texts

1932. *The Adventures of the Black Girl in Her Search for God.* London: Constable.
1934. Reprint, 1954. *The Black Girl in Search of God and Some Lesser Tales. The Standard Edition of the Works of Bernard Shaw.* London: Constable.
1977. *The Black Girl in Search of God.* In *The Portable Bernard Shaw,* edited by Stanley Weintraub. New York: Penguin; New York: Viking.
1977. *The Black Girl in Search of God and Some Lesser Tales.* Definitive text under the editorial supervision of Dan H. Laurence. Harmondsworth, England: Penguin.
2000. *The Black Girl in Search of God.* Edited by Dan H. Laurence. [Audio tape].

Other Texts

1931. Reprint, 1947. "Epistle Dedicatory to Arthur Bingham Walkley." Preface to *Man and Superman: A Comedy and a Philosophy. The Standard Edition of the Works of Bernard Shaw.* London: Constable.
1931. Reprint, 1949. *As Far As Thought Can Reach.* In *Back to Methuselah: A Metabiological Pentateuch. The Standard Edition of the Works of Bernard Shaw.* London: Constable.
1931. Reprint, 1949. *Great Catherine (Whom Glory Still Adores).* In *Heartbreak House. The Standard Edition of the Works of Bernard Shaw.* London: Constable.

1931. Reprint, 1957. "Preface on the Prospects of Christianity." Preface to *Androcles and the Lion*. In *"Androcles and the Lion," "Overruled," and "Pygmalion." The Standard Edition of the Works of Bernard Shaw*. London: Constable.

1931. Reprint, 1957. *Pygmalion: A Romance in Five Acts*. In *"Androcles and the Lion," "Overruled," and "Pygmalion." The Standard Edition of the Works of Bernard Shaw*. London: Constable.

1931. Reprint, 1964. "Preface: First-Aid to Critics." Preface to *Major Barbara*. In *"John Bull's Other Island," "How He Lied to Her Husband," and "Major Barbara." The Standard Edition of the Works of Bernard Shaw*. London: Constable.

1931. Reprint, 1964. "Preface for Politicians." Preface to *John Bull's Other Island*. In *"John Bull's Other Island," "How He Lied to Her Husband," and "Major Barbara." The Standard Edition of the Works of Bernard Shaw*. London: Constable.

1932. Reprint, 1947. Preface to *Getting Married: A Dissquisitory Play*. In *"The Doctor's Dilemma" "Getting Married," and "The Shewing-Up of Blanco Posnet." The Standard Edition of the Works of Bernard Shaw*. London: Constable.

1932. Reprint, 1947. *The Shewing-Up of Blanco Posnet*. In *"The Doctor's Dilemma," "Getting Married," and "The Shewing-Up of Blanco Posnet." The Standard Edition of the Works of Bernard Shaw*. London: Constable.

1932. Reprint, 1948. "The Quintessence of Ibsenism." In *Major Critical Essays. The Standard Edition of the Works of Bernard Shaw*. London: Constable.

1932. Reprint, 1953. "Parents and Children." Preface to *Misalliance*. In *"Misalliance," "The Dark Lady of the Sonnets," and "Fanny's First Play." The Standard Edition of the Works of Bernard Shaw*. London: Constable.

1932. Reprint, 1956. *Music in London, 1890–94*, 3 vols. *The Standard Edition of the Works of Bernard Shaw*. London: Constable.

1932. Reprint, 1961. Preface to *Saint Joan*. In *"Saint Joan: A Chronicle" and "The Apple Cart: A Political Extravaganza." The Standard Edition of the Works of Bernard Shaw*. London: Constable.

1964. *The Rationalization of Russia*. Edited by Harry M. Geduld. Bloomington: Indiana University Press.

Letters

16 November 1928. "The Irish Censorship." *Time and Tide*. [Also 17 November 1928. *Irish Statesman*]

23 January 1932. "'G.B.S.' Replies to Priest's Attack." *Cape Argus*. [Ed. comment and letter in response to Vassall-Phillips's attack]

22 February 1932. "Did Not Drive into Ditch." *Cape Times*. [Cable]

1940. Farleigh, John. *Graven Image: An Auto-biographical Textbook*. London: Macmillan. [Shaw's letters incorporated in text]

1956 (summer). "The Nun and the Dramatist," ed. "A Nun of Stanbrook." *Cornhill Magazine*. [Shaw's letters incorporated in text]

1965. *Bernard Shaw: Collected Letters, 1874–1897*. Edited by Dan H. Laurence. London: Max Reinhardt.

1972. *Bernard Shaw: Collected Letters, 1898–1910.* Edited by Dan H. Laurence. London: Max Reinhardt.

1985. *Bernard Shaw: Collected Letters, 1911–1925.* Edited by Dan H. Laurence. London: Max Reinhardt.

1988. *Bernard Shaw: Collected Letters, 1926–1950.* Edited by Dan H. Laurence. London: Max Reinhardt.

Interviews and Reports

11 January 1932. "Shaw's Greeting to S. Africa: 'Take a Good Look at Me.'" *Cape Argus.* [PVR on Shaw's arrival in Cape Town]

12 January 1932. "Breakdown of Morality." *Cape Times.* [SDI after arrival in Cape Town]

12 January 1932. "Kaapstad Verwelkom Bekende Figuur" (Cape Town welcomes well-known figure). *Burger.* [PVR (translated)]

12 January 1932. "Talk at the Tavern." *Cape Argus.* [PVR on Shaw's arrival in Cape Town]

13 January 1932. "Bernard Shaw Talks About Russia." *Cape Argus.* [PVR]

13 January 1932. "I Would Abolish Them All: Bernard Shaw's Opinion of Universities." *Cape Argus.* [PVR on address to Cape Town University Lunch Club]

14 January 1932. "'G.B.S.' Hits Out Again: The University System Attacked." *Cape Times.* [PVR on address to Cape Town University Lunch Club]

21 January 1932. "G. B. Shaw in Eikestad" (G. B. Shaw in Acorn City). *Burger.* [PVR (translated) of address to Stellenbosch University]

2 February 1932. "Shavianisms at the City Hall." *Cape Argus.* [PVR]

8 February 1932. "The Dangers of a Sun-Trap." *Cape Times.* [VR of radio broadcast]

18 March 1932. "Shaw's Final Shot at S. Africa." *Cape Argus.* [SDI]

25 May 1935. "Bernard Shaw Reis Deur Kaapstad" (Bernard Shaw passes through Cape Town). *Burger.* [PVR (translated)]

25 May 1935. "Irresponsible? Not I!" *Cape Times.* [SDI]

25 May 1935. "Mr Shaw Praises the Natives." *Star.* [SDI]

11 June 1935. "Marriage of Whites and Blacks: Startling Plan by Mr Shaw." *Daily Telegraph.* [SDI]

Secondary Sources

Betten, F. S. *The Roman Index of Forbidden Books.* Saint Louis, Mo.: Herder. 1912.

"Bishop Attacks Shaw for Story on Religion." *New York Times.* 24 December 1932.

Brande, Dorothea. "The Bishop of Everywhere's Bull." *American Review* 1, April 1933.

British Broadcasting Corporation. "The Bernard Shaw Files." (Copyright/Scriptwriter File IIb, 1941–42 and Copyright/Scriptwriter File 3, 1943–50). Written Archives Centre, Caversham Park, Reading, United Kingdom.

Brophy, Brigid. *The Adventures of God in His Search for the Black Girl.* London: Macmillan, 1973.

Burgess, Antony. "The Adventures of God." *New York Times Book Review*, 23 August 1973. [Rev. of *The Adventures of God in His Search for the Black Girl*, by Brigid Brophy]

"Cambridge Town Council Upheld Yesterday." *Times* (London), 3 February 1933. [No caption. Rep. on exclusion of *The Black Girl* from local libraries]

Corish, Patrick J. *The Irish Catholic Experience: A Historical Survey*. Wilmington, Del.: Michael Glazier, 1985.

Durrell, Lawrence. *Bromo Bombastes*. London: Caduceus, 1933.

Ervine, St John. *Bernard Shaw: His Life, Work, and Friends*. London: Constable, 1972.

"An Excluded Book." *Times* (London), 23 March 1933. [Rep. on meeting of London County Council]

"Fable on Religion Published by Shaw." *New York Times*, 6 December 1932. [Rep. on publication of *The Black Girl* in London]

Farleigh, John. *Graven Image: An Auto-biographical Textbook*. London: Macmillan, 1940.

"G.B.S." *Cape Argus*, 11 January 1932. [EL on occasion of Shaw's arrival in Cape Town]

"G.B.S. in a Motor-Car Accident." *Cape Argus*, 19 February 1932.

"G.B.S. on South Africa." *Cape Argus*, 8 February 1932. [EL on Shaw's radio broadcast]

"G.W.E." [Garrison, W. E.]. "Shaw's Flight from God." *Christian Century*, 29 March 1933. [Rev. of *The Black Girl*]

"H.A.T." "Mr Bernard Shaw Spends a Week in Knysna: A Stolen Interview." *Knysna Advertiser*, 19 February 1932.

Henderson, Archibald. *Bernard Shaw: Playboy and Prophet*. New York: Appleton, 1932.

Holroyd, Michael. *Bernard Shaw*. Vol. 3, *The Lure of Fantasy, 1918–1950*. London: Chatto and Windus, 1991.

Hugo, Leon H. "The Black Girl and Some Lesser Quests: 1932–1934." In *Shaw Offstage: The Non-Dramatic Writings*, edited by Fred D. Crawford. SHAW: *The Annual of Bernard Shaw Studies*, no. 9. University Park: Pennsylvania State University Press, 1989.

———. "Upset in a 'Suntrap': Shaw in South Africa." In *Shaw Abroad*, edited by Rodelle Weintruab. *SHAW: The Annual of Bernard Shaw Studies*, no. 5. University Park: Pennsylvania State University Press, 1985.

Hu OHS George [pseud]. "George Bernard Shaw at the Wilderness." *George and Knysna Herald*, 24 February 1932.

Hyman, Marcus. *The Adventures of the White Girl in Her Search for Knowledge*. London: Cranley and Day, 1934.

"In Search of a Better World." *Times Literary Supplement*, 4 September 1943. [Rev. of Joad's *The Adventures of the Young Soldier in Search of the Better World*]

Joad, C.E.M. *The Adventures of the Young Soldier in Search of the Better World.* Illustrated by Mervyn Peake. London: Faber and Faber, 1943.

———. *Shaw.* London: Faber and Faber, 1949.

Kazi, Mr and Mrs I. I. *Adventures of the Brown Girl (Companion to the Black Girl of Mr Bernard Shaw) in Her Search for God.* London: Stockwell, 1933; Lahore, India: Sh. Muhammed Ashraf, 1950.

Lanson, Gustave. "Voltaire at *Lés Delices* and at Ferney." In *Voltaire.* Paris: Hachette, 1906; in *Candide or the Optimist,* translated by Robert M. Adams. New York: Norton, 1966.

Laurence, Dan H. *Bernard Shaw: A Bibliography.* 2 vols. Oxford: Clarendon Press, 1983.

MacCarthy, Desmond. [caption unknown]. *Sunday Times,* probably 10 December 1932. [Rev. of *The Black Girl*]

———. "*Major Barbara:* At the Court Theatre." *Speaker,* 28 November 1905; 2 December 1905.

MacKenzie, Norman, and Jeanne, eds. *The Diary of Beatrice Webb.* Vol. 4, *The Wheel of Life, 1924–1943.* Cambridge: Belknap Press, Harvard University Press, 1985.

Matthews, W. R. *The Adventures of Gabriel in His Search for Mr Shaw: A Modest Companion for Mr Shaw's Black Girl.* Illustrated by Ruth Wood. London: Hamish Hamilton, 1933.

Maxwell, Charles Herbert. *Adventures of the White Girl in Her Search for God.* London: Lutterworth, 1933.

"Mnr Bernard Shaw, die Bekende Engelse Dramaturg en Kritikus" (Mr Bernard Shaw, the well-known dramatist and critic). *Burger,* 8 February 1932. [No caption. Comment on Shaw's radio broadcast]

"Mr George Bernard Shaw at Knysna." *George and Knysna Herald.* 2 March 1932. [Rep. on Shaw's stay in Knysna]

"Mr Hyman's Small Book Is One of Those." *Times Literary Supplement,* 17 January 1935. [No caption. Rev. of Hyman's *The Adventures of the White Girl in Her Search for Knowledge*].

"Mr Shaw on Russia." *Cape Argus,* 2 February 1932. [EL on Shaw's address in Cape Town city hall]

"Mr Shaw's 'Adventures of the Black Girl in Her Search for God' is Provoking More Than One Rejoinder." *Times Literary Supplement.* 14 September 1933. [No caption. Rev. of *The Adventures of Gabriel in His Search for Mr Shaw,* by W. R. Matthews]

"New Books: Shorter Notices." *Catholic World,* April 1933. [Rev. of *The Black Girl*]

Newton, Arvin. "Erin Go Blah." *New Republic* 74, 22 March 1933. [Rev. of *The Black Girl*]

Olivier, Sydney. *Sydney Olivier: Letters and Selected Writings.* Edited by Margaret Olivier. London: Allen and Unwin, 1948.

Olsson, ["Mr"]. "Dressing Mr Shaw's Black Girl." *Printing Trades Journal* 7, December 1932. [Rep. on printing and publishing history of *The Black Girl*]

Patch, Blanche. *Thirty Years with G.B.S.* London: Victor Gollancz, 1931.

Payne, C. *Four Men Seek God: A Reply to a Famous Author's Book.* London: Stockwell, 1934.

Pharand, Michel W. *Bernard Shaw and the French.* Gainesville: University Press of Florida, 2000.

"A Plan for Mankind." *George and Knysna Herald,* 23 March 1932. [EL on Shaw's stay in George]

"Returning Parable for Parable" *Times Literary Supplement,* 4 May 1933. [No caption. Rev. of *Adventures of the White Girl in Her Search for God,* by C. H. Maxwell]

Roberts, R. Ellis. "Shaw after Shaw." *New Statesman and Nation* 4, 10 December 1932. [Rev of *The Black Girl*]

Rolland, Romain. *Liluli.* New York: Boni and Liveright, 1920. [Translator's and illustrator's names not given.]

"A Shaw Fable." *Times* (London), 6 December 1932. [Rev. of *The Black Girl*]

"Shaw the Prophet." *Times Literary Supplement,* 8 December 1932. [Rev. of *Bernard Shaw: Playboy and Prophet,* by Archibald Henderson, and *The Black Girl*]

"Shaw Writes Parable on Mankind's Quest for God." *New York Times Book Review,* 26 February 1933. [Rev. of *The Black Girl*]

Strong, L.A.G., "Fiction." *Spectator,* 9 December 1932. [Rev. of *The Black Girl*]

Sutherland, Donald. *Further Adventures of the Black Girl in Her Search for God.* London: Shaw Society, 1999.

"Topics of the Times: Shaw Praises Bible." *New York Times,* 7 December 1932. [Rep. on publication of *The Black Girl* in London]

Vassall-Phillips, O. R. "G.B.S." *Southern Cross,* 20 January 1932.

———. "Reply to Mr Shaw." *Southern Cross,* 27 January 1932.

Voltaire (François Marie Arouet). *Candide or the Optimist.* Translated by Robert M. Adams. New York: Norton, 1966.

Wall, Mervyn. "Shaw: The Black Girl Problem," *Irish Independent Weekender,* 10 July 1993.

Ware, James M. "Shaw's 'New' Play: *The Black Girl.*" *The Shavian* (summer 1969).

Wearing, J. P., ed. *G. B. Shaw: An Annotated Bibliography of Writings about Him.* Vol. 2. Dekalb: Northern Illinois University Press, 1986.

"Wexford Beekeepers and Mr Shaw: Removal of Membership Proposed." *Times* (London), 30 December 1932. [Rep. on proposal to remove Shaw's name from list of honorary life members of Wexford Bee-keepers' Association]

"Wexford Beekeepers and Mr Shaw." *Times* (London), 27 January 1933. [Rep. on proposal to remove Shaw's name from list of honorary life members]

"Who Then Is This G.B.S.?" *Cape Argus,* 22 January 1932.

Index

Leon Hugo (1931–2002) was professor emeritus of English literature at the University of South Africa and was the author of *Bernard Shaw: Playwright and Preacher* (1971), *Edwardian Shaw: The Writer and His Age* (1999), and articles on Shavian and related subjects.